THE BEST OF SAINSBURY'S
ENTERTAINING

THE BEST OF
SAINSBURY'S
ENTERTAINING

CONTENTS

CONTRIBUTORS

Main authors: Carole Handslip, Caroline Ellwood, Wendy Godfrey

Contributing authors: Jo Turner, Rhona Newman, Norma MacMillan, Naomi Good, Clare Ferguson, Mary Reynolds, Gwyneth Loveday, Michelle Berriedale Johnson

Special Photography: Paul Williams

NOTES

Standard spoon measures are used in all recipes
1 tablespoon = one 15 ml spoon
1 teaspoon = one 5 ml spoon
All spoon measures are level.

Fresh herbs are used unless otherwise stated. If unobtainable substitute a bouquet garni of the equivalent dried herbs or used dried herbs instead but halve the quantities stated.

Use freshly ground black pepper where pepper is specified.

Size 3 eggs should be used unless otherwise stated.

Ovens should be preheated to the specified temperature.

For all recipes, quantities are given in both metric and imperial measures. Follow either set but not a mixture of both, because they are not interchangeable.

The standard alcohol measure (a 'jigger') used in the cocktail recipes is equivalent to 45 ml/1½ fl oz/ 3 tablespoons.
All cocktail recipes serve one unless otherwise stated.

Published exclusively for
J Sainsbury plc
Stamford House
Stamford Street
London SE1 9LL
by Cathay Books
Michelin House
81 Fulham Road
London SW3 6RB

First published 1985
Reprinted 1991

© Cathay Books 1985
ISBN 0 86178 335 2

Produced by Mandarin Offset
Printed and bound in Hong Kong

INTRODUCTION

Party giving can be enormous fun – whether you're holding a hectic children's party or a sumptuous celebration dinner. Without doubt some people seem to sail effortlessly through such events while others make the simplest catering operation appear such hard work. The key to success, regardless of size, formality and time of day, is always careful planning. The best laid plans undoubtedly produce the best results. But where do you begin?

The best starting point is to decide upon the type of party you wish to give – the choice is far-ranging from brunch to buffet, cocktail to celebration, children's to fondue, and includes those outdoor specialities – barbecues and garden parties. But think carefully before you choose – look at what you have got in terms of room or garden size, china, cutlery, chairs, etc and then see what you can do with them. Classic dinner parties – heavy consumers of chairs, cutlery, space and formality, have endless alternatives at hand. Consider buffet suppers or video parties for example.

The type of party you choose will unquestionably give a guide to party size. For a dinner party 6 to 8 people is the most manageable number and 30 guests as a maximum is a good rule for a cocktail or wine party.

Equalising numbers is often more difficult and often best forgotten – some of the most memorable celebrations are overwhelmingly weighted in one way or another. Do however, make a point of seating shy friends alongside the more boisterous – seating shy people together produces a weak link in conversation around a table. For the very same reason do not seat people with similar professions together otherwise business talk rules.

Having decided upon a party type and size, you can settle down to planning the menu. It is wise to limit dinner party and buffet supper courses to four – starter, main course, dessert, cheese and coffee – offering a wide choice of main course or dessert if you want to show your culinary skills.

Six to eight different nibbles or dishes will suffice for a cheese and wine or cocktail party while barbecues benefit from 3 or 4 main dishes served with a good selection of salads, vegetables and sauces followed by a simple dessert.

If you are faced with feeding large numbers and have little help, then consider serving the first course along with pre-dinner or pre-meal drinks. This will certainly help to cut down on china and cutlery clutter at the main table and some kind guest will always lend a hand with serving.

The party type and style may dictate the dishes to serve but remember to plan a menu with variety – the recipes in this book will give you lots of ideas and interspersed throughout you will find whole menu suggestions.

Advance Preparation

For ease, always shop well ahead to ensure no last minute hitches. Do as much as possible ahead of time without sacrificing flavour and freshness. Most hostesses like to have either starter or dessert, if not both, prepared well ahead, leaving only the main course requiring last minute attention.

Soups, pâtés and mousses are good starters to prepare ahead and chill (or freeze well ahead). Puddings and desserts like fruit compotes, mousses, chilled soufflés, ice creams and meringue-based desserts are also ideal for forward planning.

If you're holding a celebration party then also ensure that any celebration cake centrepiece is prepared well ahead to be simply and quickly assembled on the day.

By all means be adventurous with your entertaining, but if in doubt, or when the occasion is an important one, do have a trial run with a recipe to ensure success.

Drinks

Fruit juices and non-alcoholic punches are ideal for a children's party but do ensure that one or other is also in evidence at the more adult affairs – there will always be a number of people who for dietary or driving reasons, or those who simply through choice, prefer to stay tee-total.

Teenagers prefer something a little more exotic than the usual fizzy drink and here alcohol may be introduced with discretion. This is best done in an exotic fruit punch or cup – elaborately garnished with fruit; it has an adult image that is bound to prove popular.

For adult gatherings the choice is vast. For informal suppers where robust food is being served, consider chilled beers, lagers and cider instead of wine, and the cocktail hour has seen something of a fashionable revival over the traditional cheese and wine party.

There are no hard and fast rules about choosing wines although some with serving. Always serve white wine and rosé wine lightly chilled, and red wines at room temperature. The old adage of red wine with red meats and white wine with fish or white meats is somewhat outdated, although some wines do go better with some dishes than others. As a general guide here are some suggestions:

Thin soups and consommé: *Dry sherry*
Pâtés: *Sancerre, Vouvray*
Pasta: *Soave, Barolo*
Shellfish: *Muscadet, Pouilly-Fuissé*
Fish: *Chablis, Orvieto, dry white Rioja, Montrachet, White Burgundy, Hock, Moselle*
Chicken: *Mâcon, Graves, Médoc, Montrachet, St Emilion*
Duck: *Pommard, Mâcon, Beaujolais*
Turkey: *Beaujolais blanc, dry white Rioja*
Game: *Côtes-du-Rhône, St Emilion, Burgundy, Beaune*

Beef: *Chianti, Beaujolais, Nuits-St-Georges, Châteauneuf-du-Pâpe, Mâcon, Beaune, Côtes-du-Rhône*
Veal: *Pouilly-Fumé, Pomerol, Beaujolais*
Pork: *Mâcon, Fleurie, Portuguese red, Sancerre*
Ham: *Pouilly-Fuissé, white Burgundy*
Lamb: *Beaujolais, St Emilion, Côtes-du-Rhône, Nuits-St-Georges*
Desserts: *Tokay, Champagne (dry and sweet), Graves Doux, Vouvray, Saumur, Côtes-de-Bordeaux, Rosé-Doux, Sauternes*
Cheeses: *Orvieto, Rosé d'Anjou, Médoc, Beaune, Moselle, Soave, Rioja (red), Port, Beaujolais*

Setting the Scene

Having chosen the menu and the drinks, the time comes to set the scene. At little cost, candles produce a delightful atmosphere that is hard to beat. Their flattering effect on a room and its occupants is matched only by a spontaneous intimacy of conversation. Available in all colours and sizes, they are a must for every dinner party hostess.

Unless you are using a weathered table that does not warrant special protection then the chances are that you will use a tablecloth. Plain or fancy, the choice is unlimited from cotton and linen to lace and paper. Large bed sheets come in useful when catering for large gatherings and paper is a good option for children's parties.

Napkins offer great scope to the entertaining hostess – for informal gatherings opt for paper ones that come in almost every conceivable colour. If you use linen napkins, try folding them imaginatively for a different effect. If you find you're not at all skilful in arranging flowers or folding napkins try tucking a flower into each simply folded napkin and placing on the side plate for a professional look.

Entertaining Etiquette

Thankfully today, entertaining has few hard and fast rules and the trend is towards less formal affairs. However, there are times when one is required to present food correctly. Some areas still cause confusion so here are a few guidelines:

- Grapefruit is usually eaten with a small, pointed spoon which should already be on the plate.
- Melon is eaten with a small knife and fork or spoon and fork which should be already on the plate.
- If the number of knives, forks, spoons and glasses appears confusing then remember the invariable rule is: cutlery is used taking the outside things first and working in, glasses are in the reverse order.
- Sweet spoon (bowl to left) and sweet fork (tines to right) are set above the place mat.
- Glasses may be placed in a triangle or straight line to the top right edge of the place mat.
- Napkin is placed on side plate to the left of the place mat.

DINNER PARTIES

If you entertain regularly then you'll appreciate the care needed in devising dinner party menus that can pass all tests – the test of time when guests are late, the test of variety, colour and texture, and the test of success – will everyone share your enthusiasm?

Rules come so thick and fast for such entertaining occasions it seems remarkable that so many hostesses find the right balance. But find it they do, alternating rich, spicy dishes with blander, more subtle-tasting dishes; juggling crisp, crunchy accompaniments with creamy, melt-in-the-mouth offerings, and weighing satisfying dishes in one course with light-as-air ones in the next.

No matter whether you are a seasoned cook or a novice beginner you could do little better than to follow the seasons, choose a country's cuisine or choose a menu because of one or other of its virtues, be it vegetarian, cook-ahead or cook-together.

Confusion often exists when a country's cuisine does not fit into the conventional pattern of starter, main course and dessert. Such is true of Chinese and Indian cuisine.

With Chinese cooking, diversity and variety are the keynotes to a typical meal. However, ensure that you include a soup, a meat or poultry dish, a vegetable dish, plain-boiled rice; and at least one made-up dish like Mixed Stir-fry (see page 53) – chopsticks and fragrant China tea will set the seal on the feast.

Indian cuisine is no more of a mystery – here the emphasis is on choosing and blending different regional dishes for good effect. A traditional Indian meal begins with all the savoury dishes grouped together on the table and finishes with a light dessert or fresh fruit.

MARINATED MUSHROOMS

4 tablespoons oil
2 cloves garlic,
    crushed
1 small onion, finely
    chopped
2 bay leaves
1 thyme sprig
1 rosemary sprig
2 parsley sprigs
200 ml (⅓ pint) dry
    white wine
4-6 peppercorns
12 coriander seeds
750 g (1½ lb) button
    mushrooms
salt
chopped parsley to
    garnish

Heat the oil in a pan, add the garlic and onion and cook for 10 minutes, without browning. Stir in the herbs and wine, bring to the boil and simmer for 2 minutes. Add the peppercorns, coriander seeds, mushrooms, and salt to taste. Toss the mushrooms in the wine sauce until well coated.

Transfer to a bowl, cover and chill for 3 to 4 hours, stirring occasionally.

Spoon into a serving dish and sprinkle over the parsley. Serve with French bread or granary rolls.
Serves 6

Marinated Mushrooms; Crispy Mushrooms with Herb and Garlic Mayonnaise

CRISPY MUSHROOMS WITH HERB AND GARLIC MAYONNAISE

500 g (1 lb) button
    mushrooms
oil for deep-frying
BATTER:
125 g (4 oz) plain
    flour
pinch of salt
1 tablespoon oil
150 ml (¼ pint) water
2 egg whites
MAYONNAISE:
8 tablespoons
    mayonnaise
2 cloves garlic, crushed
2 tablespoons
    chopped parsley
1 tablespoon chopped
    basil

First, make the batter. Sift the flour and salt into a bowl, then gradually beat in the oil and water. Whisk the egg whites until very stiff, then fold into the batter.

Drop the mushrooms into the batter. Heat the oil in a deep-fryer to 190°C (375°F). Deep-fry the mushrooms in batches, lifting them from the batter to the oil, using a slotted spoon. Drain on kitchen paper and keep hot while frying the remaining mushrooms.

Mix the mayonnaise ingredients together and spoon into a bowl. Serve immediately, with the hot mushrooms.
Serves 4 to 6

STUFFED PEAR HORS D'OEUVRE

113 g (4 oz) cream cheese
1 tablespoon chopped chives
2 teaspoons chopped parsley
25 g (1 oz) walnuts, chopped
1 apple, peeled, cored and grated
2 teaspoons lemon juice
1 head of chicory
4 large ripe pears
4 slices Parma ham

Beat the cream cheese until soft. Mix in the herbs and nuts, then fold in the apple and lemon juice.

Arrange the chicory leaves on 4 individual serving plates. Peel the pears, halve and remove the cores. Spoon the filling into the core cavities and arrange two halves on each plate.

Roll up the ham slices and place in the centre. Serve immediately.
Serves 4

PROSCIUTTO CON FICHI

12 or 18 thin slices Parma ham
1 Ogen melon, seeded and cut into 4 or 6 wedges
8 or 12 ripe figs

Place the ham on individual plates and top with the melon. Cut the figs into sections, from stem end nearly through to the base. Peel back the skin and put 2 figs with each melon wedge.
Serves 4 or 6

GUACAMOLE

2 ripe avocados
1 clove garlic, crushed
½ onion, chopped
1 tablespoon lime juice
2 drops Tabasco
4 tomatoes, skinned, seeded and chopped
2 tablespoons chopped parsley
salt and pepper
1 teaspoon chilli powder
lime slices to garnish

Peel, halve and stone the avocados. Purée in an electric blender, with the garlic, onion, lime juice, Tabasco, tomatoes and parsley, until smooth. Season liberally with salt and pepper, add the chilli powder and blend again until thoroughly mixed.

Pile into a serving dish and chill for 1 hour. Garnish with lime slices and serve with melba toast.
Serves 4 to 6
NOTE: Do not chill for more than 1 hour or the guacamole may discolour.

Stuffed Pear Hors d'Oeuvre; Prosciutto con Fichi; Guacamole

PRAWN-STUFFED COURGETTES

8 small, even-sized courgettes
salt and pepper
1 tablespoon oil
1 clove garlic, crushed
2 shallots, finely chopped
4 tomatoes, skinned, seeded and chopped
2 drops Tabasco sauce
1 teaspoon crumbled thyme
250 g (8 oz) peeled prawns
25 g (1 oz) butter
25 g (1 oz) plain flour
300 ml (½ pint) milk
1 teaspoon made mustard
125 g (4 oz) Cheddar cheese, grated
1 tablespoon grated Parmesan cheese

Blanch the courgettes in boiling salted water for 2 minutes, drain and cool quickly. Halve lengthways, scoop out the flesh and chop. Arrange the shells in a shallow ovenproof dish.

Heat the oil in a pan, add the garlic and shallots and cook gently for 5 minutes. Add the tomatoes, courgette flesh, Tabasco, thyme, and salt and pepper to taste. Bring to the boil and cook, uncovered, for 25 minutes, stirring occasionally.

Add the prawns, then spoon the sauce into and over the courgettes.

Melt the butter in a pan, stir in the flour and cook for 1 minute. Gradually stir in the milk. Bring to the boil and cook, stirring, for 2 minutes. Stir in the mustard, cheeses and salt and pepper to taste.

Spoon over the courgettes and bake in a preheated hot oven, 220°C (425°F), Gas Mark 7, for 15 to 20 minutes, until golden. Serve immediately.
Serves 8

TAGLIATELLE PESTO

4 cloves garlic
50 g (2 oz) basil leaves
75 g (3 oz) Parmesan cheese, freshly grated
5-6 tablespoons olive oil
550 g (1 lb 2 oz) egg tagliatelle

Put the garlic and basil in a mortar and pound together until smooth. When the ingredients are pulped, gradually add the cheese and continue pounding until the mixture becomes oily. Add the oil, drop by drop, until a smooth sauce is obtained.

Meanwhile, cook pasta in boiling salted water for 7 to 9 minutes, or according to packet instructions. Drain well, return to the pan and pour over the pesto sauce, mixing well.

Transfer to a warmed serving dish and serve immediately, with extra Parmesan cheese.
Serves 6

Avocado with Curried Sauce

AVOCADO WITH CURRIED SAUCE

2 ripe avocados
juice of ½ lemon
SAUCE:
1-2 teaspoons curry powder
1 clove garlic, crushed
150 ml (¼ pint) mayonnaise
142 ml (5 fl oz) double cream
2 drops Tabasco sauce
salt and pepper
2 hard-boiled eggs, chopped
1 tablespoon chopped parsley
TO GARNISH:
lemon twists
parsley or basil leaves

First, make the sauce. Put the curry powder and garlic in a bowl and gradually mix in the mayonnaise and cream. Add the Tabasco sauce and season with salt and pepper to taste. Cover and leave in the refrigerator for 4 to 6 hours to allow the flavour to mellow.

Add the chopped eggs and parsley to the sauce and stir well.

Cut the avocados in half, remove the stones and sprinkle with lemon juice.

Arrange the avocado halves on 4 individual plates. Spoon the sauce into each avocado and serve immediately, garnished with lemon twists and parsley or basil leaves.
Serves 4

COLD MEAT PLATTER

125 g (4 oz) garlic
 sausage, thinly
 sliced
125 g (4 oz) Italian
 or German salami,
 thinly sliced
6-8 slices Parma
 ham, or other raw
 smoked ham,
 thinly sliced
6-8 slices honey roast
 ham, thinly sliced
6-8 slices cooked
 tongue, thinly
 sliced
TO GARNISH:
radishes and olives,
 or figs

Arrange the garlic sausage, salami,
hams and tongue on a serving platter
and garnish with radishes and olives,
or figs.
    Serve with a selection of salads.
Serves 6 to 8
NOTE: In Italy a cold platter such as
this is often served with slices of
melon, fresh figs and bread sticks.

MIXED VEGETABLE SALAD

2 tablespoons olive oil
1-2 cloves garlic,
 crushed
8 button onions
2 courgettes, sliced
125 g (4 oz) button
 mushrooms
few cauliflower
 florets
2 celery sticks,
 chopped
1 × 397 g (14 oz)
 can tomatoes
6 coriander seeds
1 bouquet garni
4 tablespoons dry
 white wine
1 tablespoon green
 peppercorns
 (optional)
salt
coriander or parsley
 sprigs to garnish

Heat the oil in a pan, add the garlic
and cook for 2 minutes, without
browning. Stir in the onions,
courgettes, mushrooms, cauliflower
and celery.
    Add the tomatoes with their juice
and bring to the boil. Add the
coriander seeds, bouquet garni, wine,
peppercorns if using, and salt to taste.
Simmer rapidly for 15 to 20 minutes,
until the vegetables are just tender
and the liquid reduced. Discard the
bouquet garni and leave to cool.
    Spoon into a serving dish and chill
until required. Garnish with
coriander or parsley to serve.
Serves 4 to 6
NOTE: If green peppercorns are
omitted, add freshly ground black
pepper to taste.

Cold Meat Platter; Mixed Vegetable Salad

PEARS WITH TARRAGON MAYONNAISE

150 ml (¼ pint)
  thick mayonnaise
4 tablespoons single
  cream
2 teaspoons tarragon
  wine vinegar
salt
cayenne pepper
2 tablespoons
  chopped tarragon
few lettuce leaves
4 ripe Comice or
  William pears
lemon twists to
  garnish

Put the mayonnaise, cream and vinegar in a bowl, with salt and cayenne pepper to taste. Stir in the chopped tarragon and mix well. Cover and set aside.

Arrange the lettuce leaves on 4 individual plates. Peel the pears and scoop out the cores with a teaspoon. Place one pear on each plate. Spoon over the tarragon mayonnaise and garnish with lemon twists. Serve chilled.
Serves 4

CHARENTAIS MELON WITH GRAPES

2 large even-sized
  Charentais melons
250 g (8 oz) small
  green grapes
150 ml (¼ pint)
  white wine
4 pieces of stem
  ginger, chopped
caster sugar

Cut the melons in half and scoop out the flesh with a melon baller, or cut into cubes. Place in a bowl. Reserve the shells.

Skin the grapes, halve and remove the pips. Add the grapes to the bowl and pour over the wine, then add the chopped ginger and sugar to taste. Mix well, cover and chill for 2 hours.

Spoon the mixture into the melon shells and serve immediately.
Serves 4

Melon, Tomato and Kiwi Vinaigrette

MELON, TOMATO AND KIWI VINAIGRETTE

2 Ogen or Charentais
  melons
4 tomatoes, skinned
3 kiwi fruit, peeled
  and sliced
1 tablespoon chopped
  mixed herbs (e.g.
  chives, mint,
  parsley)
4 tablespoons Honey
  and lemon dressing
  (see page 151)
2 tablespoons
  pumpkin seeds
  (optional)

Cut the melons in half and discard the seeds. Scoop the flesh into balls, using a melon baller, or cut into cubes; reserve the shells. Cut each tomato into 8 wedges and discard the seeds.

Place the melon in a bowl with the tomatoes, kiwi fruit and herbs. Pour over the dressing and toss well.

Spoon the mixture into the melon shells and sprinkle with pumpkin seeds if using. Serve as a light refreshing starter.
Serves 4
NOTE: Pumpkin seeds are available from healthfood stores.

TO PEEL TOMATOES

Many dinner party starter and salad recipes call for peeled tomatoes. Not as complicated to prepare as they may seem, you can speedily peel them in bulk if you cover with boiling water and leave for 45 to 60 seconds. Drain, then slit the tomato skins to peel away.

Alternatively, spear a tomato with a fork and turn over a gas flame on the hob so that the skin puckers and blisters. Allow to cool, then peel away the skin.

MELON AND MINT REFRESHER

175 g (6 oz) caster
  sugar
5 tablespoons water
small bunch of mint
1 large ripe melon
grated rind and juice
  of 2 limes or
  lemons
2 egg whites
mint sprigs to garnish

Put the sugar and water in a pan and heat until dissolved, stirring. Bring to the boil and simmer for 10 minutes. Add the mint and allow to cool.

Cut the melon flesh into chunks and purée in an electric blender. Strain the mint flavoured syrup onto the melon and add the lime or lemon rind and juice. Pour into a rigid freezerproof container, cover, seal and freeze for 2 to 3 hours, until half frozen but still soft in the centre.

Turn into a bowl and beat until smooth. Whisk the egg whites until stiff, then fold into the melon mixture. Return to the container, cover, seal and freeze until firm.

Transfer to the refrigerator 30 minutes before required, to soften slightly. Scoop into chilled individual serving dishes and garnish with mint sprigs to serve.
Serves 6

Melon and Mint Refresher; Apple and Ginger Sorbet; Tomato and Basil Sorbet

APPLE AND GINGER SORBET

4 cooking apples,
  peeled, cored and
  sliced
grated rind and juice
  of ½ lemon
3 tablespoons soft
  brown sugar
1 teaspoon ground
  ginger
6 pieces of stem
  ginger, diced
4 tablespoons ginger
  syrup (from stem
  ginger jar)
150 ml (¼ pint)
  apple juice
2 egg whites
stem ginger slices to
  garnish

Cook the apples with the lemon rind and juice until very soft. Sieve, then stir in the sugar and ground ginger and leave to cool.

Stir in the stem ginger, ginger syrup and apple juice and mix well. Pour into a rigid freezerproof container, cover, seal and freeze for about 1 hour, until the mixture is half-frozen and mushy.

Turn into a bowl and beat until smooth. Whisk the egg whites until stiff, then fold into the apple mixture. Freeze until firm.

Transfer to the refrigerator about 30 minutes before required to soften slightly. Scoop into chilled dishes and top with ginger slices.
Serves 6

TOMATO AND BASIL SORBET

1 × 1.2 litre
  (43 fl oz) can
  tomato juice
juice of ½ lemon
1 tablespoon
  Worcestershire
  sauce
2 teaspoons finely
  chopped basil
2 tablespoons dry
  white wine
2 drops Tabasco
  sauce
salt and pepper
2 egg whites
basil leaves to garnish

Mix the tomato juice, lemon juice, Worcestershire sauce, basil, wine and Tabasco together. Season with salt and pepper to taste.

Pour into a rigid freezerproof container, cover, seal and freeze for about 1½ hours, until mushy.

Turn into a bowl and whisk well. Return to the container and freeze for 1 hour, then whisk again. Whisk the egg whites until stiff, then fold into the tomato mixture. Freeze until firm.

Transfer to the refrigerator 30 minutes before required to soften slightly. Spoon into chilled dishes and serve garnished with basil.
Serves 6 to 8

RICE, TOMATO AND OLIVE SALAD

3 tablespoons long-
    grain rice
salt and pepper
4 tomatoes, skinned
50 g (2 oz) button
    mushrooms, thinly
    sliced
50 g (2 oz) black
    olives, stoned and
    halved
1 tablespoon chopped
    parsley
2 tablespoons olive oil
1 tablespoon lemon
    juice
½ clove garlic, crushed
1 teaspoon French
    mustard
2 teaspoons chopped
    basil
1 teaspoon caster
    sugar

Cook the rice in boiling salted water for 12 to 14 minutes, until tender. Drain and cool under cold running water, then drain again. Chop the tomatoes, discarding the seeds.

Put the rice, tomatoes, mushrooms and olives into a bowl and sprinkle over the parsley.

Mix the oil, lemon juice and garlic together. Blend in the mustard, basil, sugar, and salt and pepper to taste. Spoon the dressing over the rice mixture and mix well.

Transfer to a serving dish, cover and chill until required.
Serves 4 to 6

ARTICHOKES VINAIGRETTE

1 × 397 g (14 oz) can
    artichoke hearts
2 hard-boiled eggs
DRESSING:
4 tablespoons olive
    oil
1 tablespoon lemon
    juice
1 teaspoon finely
    grated lemon rind
1 tablespoon white
    wine
1 teaspoon clear
    honey
1 tablespoon each
    chopped parsley,
    oregano, thyme
    and basil
TO GARNISH:
1 tablespoon capers

Rinse the artichokes under cold running water and drain well. Cut each piece into quarters. Cut the eggs into quarters. Arrange the eggs and artichokes on a serving plate.

Mix all the dressing ingredients together, stirring well so that the herbs are evenly distributed.

Spoon the dressing over the salad and sprinkle with the capers. Cover and chill until required.
Serves 4 to 6

COURGETTE APPETIZER

1 tablespoon oil
1 clove garlic, thinly
    sliced
1 small onion, finely
    chopped
300 ml (½ pint) dry
    white wine
1 bouquet garni
1 teaspoon cumin
    seeds
350 g (12 oz)
    courgettes, sliced
salt and pepper
2 tomatoes, skinned,
    seeded and chopped
chopped herbs to
    garnish

Heat the oil in a pan, add the garlic and onion and cook for 10 minutes, without browning.

Add the wine, bring to the boil and boil rapidly until reduced by half.

Add the bouquet garni, cumin seeds, courgettes, and salt and pepper to taste. Stir well and cook for 5 to 7 minutes, until the courgettes are just tender. Remove from the heat and stir in the tomatoes. Leave until cool.

Remove the bouquet garni and chill for at least 2 hours. Serve garnished with chopped herbs.
Serves 4 to 6

PEPPERS EN SALADE

2 each red, green and
    yellow peppers
4 tablespoons olive
    oil
2 tablespoons wine
    vinegar
1 teaspoon caster
    sugar
salt and pepper
1 teaspoon Meaux
    mustard
1 × 50 g (1¾ oz)
    can anchovy fillets,
    drained
black olives to
    garnish

Preheat the grill to very hot. Grill the peppers as close to the heat as possible until the skin is charred on all sides. Rub off the skins under cold running water.

Halve the peppers and remove the cores and seeds. Slice into thin strips and arrange on a plate.

Mix the oil, vinegar and sugar together with salt and pepper to taste. Add the mustard and mix well.

Spoon the dressing over the peppers. Arrange the anchovy fillets in a lattice pattern over the top and garnish with olives.

Cover and chill until required.
Serves 4 to 6

*Rice, Tomato and Olive Salad; Artichokes Vinaigrette;
Peppers en Salade*

SMOKED SALMON PÂTÉ

250 g (8 oz) smoked
  salmon trimmings
50 g (2 oz) unsalted
  butter, softened
6 tablespoons lemon
  juice
salt
cayenne pepper
1 drop Tabasco sauce
1 tablespoon chopped
  chives
1 tablespoon chopped
  parsley
lemon slices to
  garnish

Remove any bones and skin from the salmon and mince or chop finely.

Cream the butter and 2 tablespoons of the lemon juice together, then beat in the salmon, and season with salt and cayenne pepper to taste. Add the Tabasco and remaining lemon juice and mix until the pâté is thick and creamy. Stir in the chives and parsley. Cover and chill until required.

Spoon the pâté into 4 individual dishes and garnish with lemon slices. Serve with hot buttered toast.
Serves 4

SMOKED MACKEREL PÂTÉ

250 g (8 oz) smoked
  mackerel fillets
25 g (1 oz) unsalted
  butter
1 small onion, finely
  chopped
2 tablespoons flour
150 ml (¼ pint)
  milk
2 teaspoons lemon
  juice
1 tablespoon dry
  white wine
salt and pepper
142 ml (5 fl oz)
  double cream,
  lightly whipped
TO GARNISH:
few lettuce leaves
cucumber twists

Remove the skin and bones from the mackerel and flake the fish. Heat the butter in a pan, add the onion and cook for 5 to 7 minutes, without browning.

Stir in the flour and cook for 2 minutes. Gradually stir in the milk and cook, stirring, for 1 minute. Transfer to a bowl.

Stir in the lemon juice and wine and season liberally with salt and pepper. Add the fish to the sauce and beat until smooth. Fold in the cream. Cover and chill until required.

Spoon the mixture into 4 individual dishes lined with lettuce leaves. Decorate with cucumber twists and serve with hot buttered toast or French bread.
Serves 4
NOTE: This tasty pâté can alternatively be made with kipper fillets. Add 1 tablespoon finely chopped parsley with the onion for additional flavour.

Terrine de Canard

TERRINE DE CANARD

1 × 1.5 kg (3 lb)
  oven-ready duck,
  skin and bones
  removed
500 g (1 lb) minced
  pork
350 g (12 oz) minced
  veal
1 clove garlic, crushed
1 tablespoon Worcester-
  shire sauce
juice of 1 orange
2 teaspoons dried
  mixed herbs
150 ml (¼ pint) dry
  red wine
salt and pepper
10 rashers streaky
  bacon, derinded
1 tablespoon brandy
TO GARNISH:
orange twists
watercress sprigs

Dice the duck meat and mix with the pork and veal. Add the garlic, Worcestershire sauce, orange juice, herbs, wine, and salt and pepper to taste. Cover and chill overnight.

Using a sharp knife, stretch the bacon rashers and use to line the base and sides of a 1 kg (2 lb) terrine or loaf tin. Press the meat mixture into the tin, sprinkle with the brandy and cover with foil.

Place in a roasting pan and pour in enough boiling water to come half-way up the sides of the pan. Cook in a preheated moderate oven, 180°C (350°F), Gas Mark 4, for 1½ to 1¾ hours.

Leave until cold then turn out onto a serving dish. Serve garnished with orange twists and watercress.
Serves 8

COUNTRY PÂTÉ

*500 g (1 lb) streaky
bacon rashers*
*125 g (4 oz) fresh
white breadcrumbs*
2 eggs
*150 ml (¼ pint) dry
red wine*
2 cloves garlic, crushed
*350 g (12 oz) belly
pork, minced*
*350 g (12 oz) pork
livers, chopped*
*500 g (1 lb) chicken
livers, chopped*
*1 teaspoon each
chopped thyme
and sage*
*1 tablespoon chopped
parsley*
grated nutmeg
salt and pepper
*parsley sprigs to
garnish*

Remove the rind from the bacon rashers and use half to line the base and sides of a large terrine or loaf tin, stretching them to fit if necessary. Chop the rest of the bacon and mix with the remaining ingredients, adding nutmeg, salt and pepper to taste.

Turn into the prepared dish, press down firmly and cover with buttered greaseproof paper and foil. Place in a bain-marie and bake in a preheated moderate oven, 160°C (325°F), Gas Mark 3, for 2 to 2½ hours.

Place a weight on top of the terrine and leave to cool, then chill. Turn out and garnish with parsley. Serve sliced, with Melba toast.
Serves 10 to 12

TERRINE OF CHICKEN

40 g (1½ oz) butter
*50 g (2 oz) button
mushrooms,
chopped*
*1 clove garlic,
roughly chopped*
*500 g (1 lb) chicken
livers, chopped*
*3 tablespoons dry red
wine*
*1 teaspoon chopped
thyme*
salt
1 tablespoon brandy
*1 tablespoon single
cream*
*250 g (8 oz) boned
chicken, thinly
sliced*
*2 tablespoons green
peppercorns*
*lettuce leaves to
garnish*

Melt half the butter in a pan, add the mushrooms and cook for 2 minutes. Remove with a slotted spoon and set aside. Add the remaining butter and garlic to the pan; cook for 1 minute. Add the chicken livers and cook for 5 minutes. Add the wine, thyme, and salt to taste. Cook for 15 minutes.

Work the mixture in an electric blender until smooth, then stir in the mushrooms, brandy and cream.

Spoon a thin layer of liver mixture into a lightly greased 500 g (1 lb) terrine. Cover with a layer of chicken, then sprinkle with a few peppercorns. Repeat layers until all the ingredients are used, finishing with liver mixture. Cover with a lid or foil.

Stand the dish in a roasting pan containing enough boiling water to come halfway up the sides of the dish. Cook in a preheated moderate oven, 180°C (350°F), Gas Mark 4, for 1 to 1¼ hours. Cool, then chill until required. Garnish with lettuce and serve with toast.
Serves 6 to 8

PÂTÉS, MOUSSES AND TERRINES

Scooped, potted or sliced there is a pâté, mousse or terrine to suit every dinner party occasion – and they have the added bonus that many can be made well ahead.

If you plan to make a pâté in advance then it is worthwhile topping with a little clarified butter so that it will keep moist. To clarify butter, melt in a pan over a low heat. Cook for ½ minute without colouring and remove surface scum. Strain through a muslin-lined sieve into a bowl. Pour again into another bowl leaving behind any settled sediment. Pour over the pâté and chill to set.

Ring the changes in serving such popular starters by adding unusual accompaniments – try crispbreads and crackers instead of the usual toast fingers; flavoured breakaway bread boasting a garlic, lemon, herb or mustard butter; or impress with light-as-air Melba toast.

To make Melba toast, simply toast both sides of a piece of bread. Quickly slice horizontally again using a sharp knife to make two very thin slices. Halve each slice diagonally and quickly toast on the uncooked sides – the edges will curl to produce fragile 'scoops' of Melba toast.

Terrine of Chicken

TUNA PÂTÉ

2 × 198 g (7 oz) cans
  tuna fish, drained
250 g (8 oz) unsalted
  butter, softened
25 g (1 oz) stoned
  green olives
pepper
TO GARNISH:
lemon slices
parsley sprigs

Place all the ingredients in an electric blender or food processor, adding pepper to taste.

Work until smooth, transfer to a 900 ml (1½ pint) dish and chill for about 2 hours, or until required.

Serve, garnished with lemon slices and parsley sprigs, accompanied by wholewheat toast.

Serves 4 to 6

TURKEY LIVER PÂTÉ

125 g (4 oz) butter
1 × 227 g (8 oz) tub
  frozen turkey
  livers, thawed and
  trimmed
1 onion, chopped
1 clove garlic, crushed
1 tablespoon sweet
  sherry
50 g (2 oz) shelled
  pistachio nuts,
  coarsely chopped
salt and pepper
watercress sprigs to
  garnish

Melt 75 g (3 oz) of the butter in a small pan, add the turkey livers and fry for 5 minutes, turning frequently. Set aside. Fry the onion and garlic in the fat remaining in the pan until softened; add to the livers.

Melt the remaining butter in the pan and stir in the sherry, scraping up the sediment. Place in an electric blender or food processor with the livers and onion and work until smooth.

Stir in the nuts and add salt and pepper to taste.

Transfer to a dish, cover and leave to mature in the refrigerator for 2 days. Garnish with watercress and serve with wholewheat toast.

Serves 4

GARNISHES

Dinner party starters should be garnished with style. Spend a little extra time on decorations – instead of the usual chopped or sprig of herbs, try making citrus fruit or cucumber twists, gherkin fans, delicate herb bundles or bows, or serve on a finely shredded nest of seasonal salad vegetables. Crisp yet delicate Chinese leaves, colourful crimson radicchio, soft and aromatic corn salad or wonderful wispy endive – all sliced paper thin make interesting and unusual salad beds.

Tuna Pâté; Turkey Liver Pâté; Garbanzos Pâté

SALMON MOUSSE

300 ml (½ pint) milk
3 white peppercorns
1 bay leaf
1 blade mace
1 onion, stuck with
  2 cloves
1 small carrot
1 envelope gelatine,
  dissolved in
  2 tablespoons water
150 ml (¼ pint) dry
  white wine
¼ cucumber, sliced
40 g (1½ oz) butter
25 g (1 oz) plain
  flour
2 eggs, separated
2 × 99 g (3½ oz)
  cans red salmon,
  drained
salt and pepper
2-3 tablespoons single
  cream
TO GARNISH:
lemon twist
gherkin slices
olive slices

Put the milk in a pan with the peppercorns, bay leaf, mace, onion and carrot and leave to infuse over very low heat for 15 minutes.

Add the dissolved gelatine to the wine. Pour a little onto the base of a 900 ml (1½ pint) mould and leave to set. Arrange cucumber slices on top, cover with a little wine and leave to set; keep remaining wine warm to prevent setting.

Strain the milk into a pan and add the butter and flour. Bring to the boil, whisking constantly. Remove from the heat, cool slightly and beat in the egg yolks, one at a time. Add the salmon, and salt and pepper to taste.

Work the mixture in an electric blender or food processor until smooth. Stir in the remaining wine and the cream. Whisk the egg whites until stiff and fold into the mixture. Turn into the mould and chill for 2 hours or until set. Turn out and serve garnished with lemon, gherkin and olive slices.
Serves 6

GARBANZOS PÂTÉ

1 × 400 g (14 oz)
  can chick peas,
  drained
125 g (4 oz) salami,
  chopped
2 cloves garlic,
  crushed
salt and pepper
4-6 basil or parsley
  sprigs, chopped

Place the chick peas, salami and garlic in an electric blender or food processor and work until smooth. Season well with salt and pepper and stir in half of the basil or parsley.

Transfer to individual dishes and chill until required.

Garnish with remaining herbs and serve with Melba toast (see note on page 19) or warm pitta bread.
Serves 4

CHICKEN AND VEGETABLE TERRINE

125 g (4 oz) cooked
  chicken
350 g (12 oz)
  skimmed milk soft
  cheese
3 eggs
salt and white pepper
125 g (4 oz) spinach,
  cooked
125 g (4 oz) carrots,
  cooked
TO SERVE:
Tomato and Orange
  Sauce (see page
  151)
few chives, chopped

Place the chicken, one third of the cheese and one egg in an electric blender or food processor and work to a purée. Season with salt and pepper to taste. Repeat this process twice, using the spinach, then the carrots, in place of the chicken.

Grease a 500 g (1 lb) loaf tin and spoon in the chicken mixture. Carefully spoon over the carrot mixture, then the spinach mixture.

Place the tin in a roasting pan half-filled with water and cook in a preheated moderate oven, 160°C (325°F), Gas Mark 3, for 1 hour.

Leave to cool, then turn out onto a serving plate and surround with the sauce, sprinkled with chives.
Serves 6

Chicken and Vegetable Terrine

SEAFOOD SAFFRON SOUP

2 large onions,
    chopped
250 g (8 oz)
    potatoes, diced
600 ml (1 pint) milk
300 ml (½ pint) fish
    or chicken stock
750 g (1½ lb) white
    fish fillets
4 shelled scallops,
    roughly chopped
120 ml (4 fl oz)
    white wine
1 teaspoon powdered
    saffron
salt and pepper
125 g (4 oz) peeled
    prawns
142 ml (5 fl oz)
    double cream
few unshelled cooked
    prawns to garnish

Put the onions and potatoes in a pan, add the milk and stock and bring to the boil. Cook for 15 minutes, until soft. Cool slightly, then sieve or work in an electric blender or food processor until smooth.

Cut the fish into 4 cm (1½ inch) pieces. Return the soup to the pan and add the fish and scallops. Cook gently for about 10 minutes, until tender. Stir in the wine and saffron, and season with salt and pepper to taste.

Stir in the prawns and cream and serve immediately, garnished with prawns.
Serves 4 to 6

MUSSEL CHOWDER

1 kg (2 lb) mussels
    in shells
250 g (8 oz) white
    fish fillets, skinned
40 g (1½ oz) butter
1 onion, chopped
2 celery sticks, chopped
1 clove garlic, crushed
25 g (1 oz) plain
    flour
900 ml (1½ pints)
    fish stock
150 ml (¼ pint) dry
    white wine
salt and white pepper
1 bouquet garni
50 g (2 oz) long-
    grain rice, cooked
2 strands saffron
2 egg yolks
3 tablespoons cream
2 tablespoons
    chopped parsley

Scrub the mussels clean and cut the fish into 4 cm (1½ inch) pieces.

Melt the butter in a pan, add the onion, celery and garlic and cook for 2 minutes, without browning. Stir in the flour and cook for 2 minutes. Gradually stir in the stock and bring to the boil. Stir in the wine, and season with salt and pepper to taste.

Add the fish, bouquet garni and mussels. Cover and cook for 5 to 7 minutes or until the fish is tender and the mussel shells have opened; discard any that do not. Stir in the rice and saffron, and heat through. Discard the bouquet garni.

Blend the egg yolks and cream together. Pour 1 tablespoon hot soup onto the egg mixture and mix well.

Remove the soup from the heat and stir in the blended mixture with the parsley. Serve immediately.
Serves 6

SWEETCORN AND PRAWN SOUP

2 teaspoons finely
    chopped root
    ginger
1 tablespoon dry
    sherry
250 g (8 oz) frozen
    peeled prawns,
    thawed
900 ml (1½ pints)
    chicken stock
1 × 326 g (11½ oz)
    can sweetcorn
salt
50 g (2 oz) lean
    ham, diced
1 tablespoon chopped
    chives

Mix the ginger, sherry and prawns together. Bring the stock to the boil, then stir in the prawn mixture. Drain the sweetcorn and add to the pan with salt to taste. Cook for 2 minutes, stirring occasionally.

Sprinkle with the ham and chives and serve immediately.
Serves 4 to 6

Iced Tomato and Basil Soup

ICED TOMATO AND BASIL SOUP

1 tablespoon oil
1 large onion, chopped
1 clove garlic, crushed
25 g (1 oz) flour
1 kg (2 lb) ripe
    tomatoes
1 tablespoon Worcester-
    shire sauce
2 drops Tabasco
    sauce
250 ml (8 fl oz) dry
    white wine
1 tablespoon tomato
    purée
salt and pepper
3 tablespoons
    chopped basil
TO GARNISH:
6 tablespoons double
    cream, whipped
chopped chives

Heat the oil in a large pan, add the onion and garlic and cook for 5 minutes, without browning. Stir in the flour and cook, stirring, for 2 minutes.

Chop the tomatoes roughly and add to the pan. Cover and cook gently for 20 minutes, stirring occasionally. Add the Worcester and Tabasco sauces, wine, tomato purée, and salt and pepper to taste. Bring to the boil, cover and simmer for 30 minutes. Cool slightly.

Sieve or work in an electric blender until smooth then strain into a bowl.

Leave to cool, then stir in the basil and chill for several hours.

Pour into individual soup bowls. Top each with a swirl of cream and chopped chives. Serve immediately.
Serves 6

LEFT: *Seafood Saffron Soup; Mussel Chowder*

MUSHROOM SOUP WITH MADEIRA

75 g (3 oz) butter
1 large onion, finely
    chopped
500 g (1 lb)
    mushrooms, finely
    chopped
25 g (1 oz) plain
    flour
900 ml (1½ pints)
    chicken stock
salt and pepper
120 ml (4 fl oz) dry
    Madeira
142 ml (5 fl oz)
    double cream
chopped parsley to
    garnish

Melt the butter in a large pan, add the onion and cook for 20 minutes or until evenly browned. Add the mushrooms and cook for 2 minutes.

Stir in the flour and cook for 1 minute. Gradually stir in the stock, then season with salt and pepper to taste. Bring to the boil, cover and simmer for 10 minutes.

Stir in the Madeira and cream and heat through gently. Serve immediately, garnished with parsley.
Serves 4 to 6

CHILLED ALMOND SOUP

15 g (½ oz) butter
1 small onion, finely
  chopped
25 g (1 oz) plain
  flour
900 ml (1½ pints)
  chicken stock
175 g (6 oz) flaked
  almonds
1 bay leaf
salt
142 ml (5 fl oz)
  double cream
toasted flaked
  almonds to garnish

Melt the butter in a large pan, add the onion and cook for 5 minutes until transparent.

Stir in the flour and cook for 1 minute, without browning. Gradually add the stock, stirring constantly. Add the almonds, bay leaf and salt to taste. Bring to the boil, cover and simmer for 20 minutes.

Leave until cool, then remove the bay leaf. Sieve or work in an electric blender until smooth. Transfer to a bowl and chill for 2 to 3 hours.

Just before serving, stir in the cream and sprinkle over the toasted almonds.

Serves 4 to 6

Iced Avocado Soup; Prawn Bisque; Chilled Almond Soup

ICED AVOCADO SOUP

2 ripe avocados
juice of ½ lemon
2 × 411 g (14½ oz)
  cans chicken
  consommé
142 ml (5 fl oz)
  double cream
pinch of cayenne
  pepper
2 drops Tabasco
  sauce
salt and white pepper
TO GARNISH:
lemon slices
parsley sprigs

Cut the avocados in half lengthwise, remove the stones and scoop out all the flesh. Mix with the lemon juice and sieve or work in an electric blender or food processor until smooth.

Transfer to a bowl and stir in the remaining ingredients, with salt and pepper to taste. Chill for several hours before serving.

Garnish with lemon slices and parsley sprigs. Serve with garlic and herb bread.

Serves 4 to 6

PRAWN BISQUE

25 g (1 oz) butter
1 onion, finely
  chopped
1 clove garlic, crushed
25 g (1 oz) plain
  flour
1 × 397 g (14 oz) and
  1 × 227 g (8 oz)
  can tomatoes
juice of ½ lemon
1 bouquet garni
salt and pepper
2 tablespoons dry
  white wine
250 g (8 oz) cod or
  haddock fillets, cut
  into 2.5 cm
  (1 inch) pieces
250 g (8 oz) peeled
  prawns, roughly
  chopped

Melt the butter in a large pan, add the onion and garlic and cook for 5 minutes, without browning.

Stir in the flour and cook for 2 minutes. Gradually stir in the tomatoes, with their juice, and the lemon juice. Add the bouquet garni, and salt and pepper to taste. Bring to the boil, cover and simmer for 25 minutes.

Remove the bouquet garni. Sieve or work in an electric blender until smooth.

Return to the pan, stir in the wine, fish and prawns and cook for 5 to 7 minutes, until the fish is tender.

Transfer to a bowl and leave to cool, then chill for several hours before serving.

Serves 6

CHILLED WATERCRESS SOUP

25 g (1 oz) butter
2 leeks, thinly sliced
1 small onion,
    chopped
250 g (8 oz) potato,
    diced
2 bunches of
    watercress
600 ml (1 pint)
    chicken stock
salt and pepper
300 ml (½ pint)
    milk
croûtons to garnish

Melt the butter in a pan, add the leeks and onion and fry for 5 minutes, without browning. Add the potato and cook for 2 minutes.

Meanwhile, remove the tough stalks from the watercress and roughly chop the leaves. Add to the pan with the stock, and salt and pepper to taste. Bring to the boil, then cover and simmer for 25 to 30 minutes.

Sieve or work in an electric blender until smooth. Pour into a bowl and stir in the milk. Chill for several hours before serving.

Serve garnished with croûtons.
Serves 4 to 6

SUMMER VEGETABLE SOUP

8 large ripe tomatoes
2 cloves garlic
½ small onion
½ cucumber
1 green pepper, cored
    and seeded
1 red pepper, cored
    and seeded
1 thyme sprig
1 basil sprig
2 parsley sprigs
6 tablespoons olive oil
4 tablespoons lemon
    juice
600 ml (1 pint)
    tomato juice,
    chilled
few drops of Tabasco
    sauce
TO SERVE:
garlic-flavoured
    croûtons
black olives
capers

Chop the tomatoes, garlic, onion, cucumber and peppers roughly. Put these ingredients into an electric blender and blend until smooth. Add the herbs and blend again.

Strain into a bowl and chill for several hours.

Just before serving, mix the olive oil and lemon juice together. Add the tomato juice and Tabasco, and gradually stir this mixture into the soup. Garnish with croûtons and serve black olives and capers as accompaniments.
Serves 6

Chilled Watercress Soup; Summer Vegetable Soup

SWEET PEPPER SOUP

40 g (1½ oz) butter
1 large onion, finely
    chopped
1 clove garlic, crushed
25 g (1 oz) plain
    flour
900 ml (1½ pints)
    chicken stock
500 g (1 lb) red
    peppers, cored,
    seeded and chopped
1 dried red chilli,
    chopped
250 g (8 oz)
    tomatoes, skinned,
    seeded and chopped
1 teaspoon chopped
    thyme
chopped chives to
    garnish

Melt the butter in a large pan, add the onion and garlic and fry gently for 2 minutes. Stir in the flour and cook for a further 2 minutes. Gradually add the stock, stirring constantly, and bring to the boil.

Add the red peppers, chilli, tomatoes and thyme. Cover and simmer for 20 to 25 minutes, until the vegetables are tender. Cool slightly.

Sieve or work in an electric blender until smooth. Return to the pan and heat through. Garnish with chives before serving.

Serves 6

GARLIC SOUP

2 tablespoons olive
    oil
24 cloves garlic,
    peeled
900 ml (1½ pints)
    beef or chicken
    stock
1 bouquet garni
pinch of grated
    nutmeg
1 blade mace
salt and pepper
3 egg yolks
6-8 slices French
    bread
TO FINISH:
chopped parsley
grated Parmesan
    cheese

Heat the oil in a large pan, add the whole garlic cloves and fry, without browning, for 10 minutes.

Stir in the stock and add the bouquet garni, nutmeg, mace, and salt and pepper to taste. Bring to the boil, cover and simmer for 20 minutes.

Blend the egg yolks with 2 tablespoons of the soup. Strain remaining soup and return to the pan. Bring to the boil, then set aside for 2 minutes.

Meanwhile, toast the bread on both sides; place in individual soup bowls.

Pour the egg yolk mixture into the soup, stirring constantly. Ladle into the bowls and serve at once, garnished with chopped parsley. Hand the Parmesan cheese separately.

Serves 6 to 8

Garlic Soup; Sweet Pepper Soup; Aubergine and Crab Soup

AUBERGINE AND CRAB SOUP

1 tablespoon oil
2 large onions,
    chopped
2 cloves garlic,
    crushed
4 large aubergines,
    peeled and chopped
1 × 397 g (14 oz)
    can tomatoes
300 ml (½ pint)
    chicken stock
1 tablespoon tomato
    purée
1 bouquet garni
120 ml (4 fl oz) dry
    white wine
salt and pepper
1 × 177 g (6 oz) can
    crabmeat, drained
    and flaked
chopped parsley to
    garnish

Heat the oil in a pan, add the onions and garlic and cook for 5 to 7 minutes, without browning. Stir in the aubergines and the tomatoes with their juice. Bring slowly to the boil and stir in the stock, tomato purée, bouquet garni and wine. Season with salt and pepper to taste. Cover and simmer for 30 minutes, until the vegetables are very tender. Discard the bouquet garni and cool slightly.

Sieve or work in an electric blender until smooth. Return to the pan, stir in the crabmeat and bring to the boil.

Serve immediately, garnished with chopped parsley.

Serves 6

MULLIGATAWNY SOUP

250 g (8 oz) lentils
2 tablespoons oil
2 large onions,
    chopped
1 tablespoon curry
    powder
2 cloves garlic, crushed
1 red pepper, cored,
    seeded and chopped
3 dried chillies,
    chopped
1.2 litres (2 pints)
    chicken stock
25 g (1 oz) seedless
    raisins
250 g (8 oz)
    tomatoes, skinned,
    seeded and chopped
1 tablespoon tomato
    purée
salt and pepper
saffron rice to garnish
    (optional)

Soak the lentils in cold water overnight; rinse and drain.

Heat the oil in a pan, add the onions and fry until browned.

Stir in the curry powder and cook for 2 minutes, stirring occasionally. Add the garlic, lentils and remaining ingredients, with salt and pepper to taste. Bring to the boil, cover and simmer for 1½ hours. Cool slightly.

Sieve or work in an electric blender until smooth. Return to the pan and heat through.

Serve hot, garnished with saffron rice if liked.
Serves 8
NOTE: To make saffron rice, cook rice in boiling salted water with a few saffron strands added, until tender.

Mulligatawny Soup; Breton Onion Soup; Curried Parsnip Soup

BRETON-STYLE ONION SOUP

40 g (1½ oz) butter
500 g (1 lb) strong
    onions, sliced
250 g (8 oz)
    potatoes, diced
1.2 litres (2 pints)
    beef stock
1 bouquet garni
salt and pepper
oil for shallow frying
4 cloves garlic, sliced
1 small French loaf,
    sliced into 1 cm
    (½ inch) rounds
50 g (2 oz) Cheddar
    cheese, grated

Melt the butter in a pan, add the onions and cook gently for 30 minutes or until golden brown.

Add the potatoes, stock, bouquet garni, and salt and pepper to taste. Bring to the boil, cover and simmer for 15 to 20 minutes, until the potatoes are tender. Remove the bouquet garni.

Heat the oil in a frying pan with the garlic, add the bread and fry until golden brown on both sides; drain.

Ladle the soup into individual heatproof bowls. Float 1 or 2 pieces of bread in each bowl and sprinkle with the cheese. Place under a preheated hot grill until the cheese is bubbling. Serve immediately.
Serves 6 to 8

CURRIED PARSNIP SOUP

50 g (2 oz) butter
1 teaspoon curry
    powder
2 large onions,
    chopped
750 g (1½ lb)
    parsnips, chopped
600 ml (1 pint)
    chicken stock
salt and white pepper
300 ml (½ pint)
    milk
142 ml (5 fl oz)
    single cream
1 red apple, diced and
    tossed in lemon
    juice, to garnish

Melt the butter in a large pan, stir in the curry powder and cook for 2 minutes. Add the onions and parsnips and cook gently for 5 minutes, stirring occasionally. Add the stock, and salt and pepper to taste.

Bring to the boil and cook for 25 to 30 minutes, until the vegetables are tender. Cool slightly.

Sieve or work in an electric blender until smooth. Return to the pan and add the milk and cream. Bring to the boil, stirring; check the seasoning and serve immediately, garnished with the apple.
Serves 6 to 8

TROUT WITH HERBS

4 tablespoons
    wholewheat flour
½ teaspoon salt
¼ teaspoon pepper
4 trout, cleaned
3 tablespoons olive oil
TO FINISH:
25 g (1 oz) butter
juice of ½ lemon
1 tablespoon chopped
    mixed herbs
    (parsley, chives
    and thyme)
salt and pepper

Mix together the flour, salt and pepper and use to coat the trout. Heat the oil in a heavy frying pan, add the fish and fry for 5 to 6 minutes on each side until golden brown. Place on a warmed serving dish and keep hot.

Wipe the frying pan with kitchen paper. Add the butter and cook until golden brown. Quickly add the lemon juice, herbs, and salt and pepper to taste. Pour over the trout and serve immediately.
Serves 4

Trout with Herbs

SCALLOPS WITH GARLIC AND PARSLEY

75 g (3 oz) butter
3 cloves garlic
12 fresh scallops,
    shelled, or frozen
    scallops, thawed
2 tablespoons
    chopped parsley
salt and pepper

Melt the butter in a pan, add the garlic and fry until browned; discard.

Add the coral and white scallop flesh to the pan and cook for 5 minutes. Sprinkle in the parsley, and salt and pepper to taste. Pile into warmed individual serving dishes and serve immediately.
Serves 4

TROUT WITH ALMONDS

4 trout, cleaned, with
    heads and tails
    intact
salt and pepper
75 g (3 oz) butter
50 g (2 oz) flaked
    almonds
juice of 1 lemon
TO GARNISH:
lemon slices
parsley sprigs

Season the fish with salt and pepper. Melt the butter in a frying pan, add the trout and fry for 6 minutes on each side until golden and cooked through. Arrange on a warmed serving dish and keep hot.

Fry the almonds in the butter remaining in the pan until golden. Add the lemon juice and spoon over the fish. Garnish with lemon and parsley and serve immediately.
Serves 4

SALMON STEAK WITH VERMOUTH

25 g (1 oz) fresh
    breadcrumbs
salt and pepper
4 salmon steaks
50 g (2 oz) butter
2 teaspoons lemon
    juice
4 tablespoons dry
    vermouth
lemon slices and
    parsley sprig to
    garnish

Mix the breadcrumbs with salt and pepper and use to coat the fish steaks. Melt the butter in a frying pan. Add the fish steaks and brown on both sides. Transfer the steaks to a baking dish and pour over the butter from the pan. Sprinkle with the lemon juice and vermouth.

Bake in a preheated moderately hot oven, 190°C (375°F), Gas Mark 5, for 15 to 20 minutes. Garnish with the lemon slices and parsley.
Serves 4

MEDITERRANEAN FISH STEW

Use a selection of the following for contrast in textures and flavours: cod or haddock, plaice or sole, red or grey mullet, bream or mackerel, scallops or mussels, crab and prawns.

1.5 kg (3 lb) assorted fish, cleaned
2 tablespoons olive oil
1 large onion, chopped
2 leeks, chopped
4 cloves garlic, crushed
500 g (1 lb) tomatoes, skinned and chopped
1 bay leaf
1 bouquet garni
300 ml (½ pint) dry white wine
few saffron strands
salt and pepper
1 loaf French bread, sliced and toasted
chopped parsley to garnish

Remove the heads, bones and skin from the fish; put these in a pan and cover with water. Bring to the boil and simmer for 15 minutes. Strain and reserve the stock. Cut the fish into pieces.

Heat the oil in a large pan, add the onion and leeks and fry until golden. Add the garlic, tomatoes, herbs and wine. Add the fish except the prawns and crab. Pour in the stock, adding water to cover if necessary. Add saffron, salt and pepper to taste. Bring to the boil, cover and simmer for 10 minutes. Add the prawns and crab; cook for 2 minutes.

Arrange the toast in the base of a large tureen or dish, lift the fish from the pan and pile on top. Boil the stock rapidly for 2 minutes, then strain over the fish. Sprinkle liberally with parsley and serve at once.
Serves 6 to 8

HERRINGS LYONNAISE

50 g (2 oz) butter
2 large onions, sliced
2 tablespoons plain flour
salt and pepper
4 herrings, cleaned
2 tablespoons dry white wine
2 tablespoons chopped parsley

Melt the butter in a pan, add the onions and fry until golden. Drain on kitchen paper.

Season the flour with salt and pepper and use to coat the herrings. Fry in the fat remaining in the pan until well browned. Arrange on a warmed serving dish.

Return the onions to the pan and pour in the wine. Cook for 2 minutes. Sprinkle in the parsley, pour over the herrings and serve.
Serves 4

Mediterranean Fish Stew; Herrings Lyonnaise

CREOLE-STYLE PRAWNS

1 tablespoon oil
1 large onion, chopped
1 clove garlic, crushed
2 celery sticks, thinly
    sliced
350 g (12 oz)
    tomatoes, skinned
1 green pepper, cored
    and seeded
salt and pepper
4 tablespoons dry
    white wine
1 tablespoon tomato
    purée
500 g (1 lb) peeled
    prawns
2 drops Tabasco sauce
1 teaspoon Worcester-
    shire sauce
1 tablespoon chopped
    parsley

Heat the oil in a pan, add the onion and garlic and fry until lightly browned. Add the celery and cook for 2 minutes.

Cut the tomatoes in half, remove the seeds and chop the flesh. Finely chop the green pepper. Add the tomatoes and pepper to the pan with salt and pepper to taste. Stir in the wine and tomato purée. Bring to the boil and simmer, uncovered, for 20 minutes.

Stir in the prawns, Tabasco and Worcestershire sauces. Simmer for 5 minutes, then stir in the parsley. Serve immediately, garnished with lemon twists and celery leaves, if liked. Serve with rice or pasta and a green salad.
Serves 6

MEDITERRANEAN SEAFOOD

15 g (½ oz) butter
2 shallots, chopped
150 ml (¼ pint) dry
    white wine
2 tablespoons dry
    sherry
1 teaspoon French
    mustard
pinch of cayenne
dash of Worcester-
    shire sauce
142 ml (5 fl oz)
    double cream
2 × 177 g (6 oz)
    cans crabmeat,
    drained
250 g (8 oz) peeled
    prawns
salt and pepper
2-3 tablespoons grated
    Parmesan cheese

Melt the butter in a pan, add the shallots and cook until softened, without browning. Pour in the wine and sherry, bring to the boil and boil rapidly until thickened and reduced by half.

Stir in the mustard, cayenne and Worcestershire sauce and cook for 2 minutes. Add the cream, bring to the boil, and boil for 5 to 7 minutes, stirring occasionally, until thickened.

Remove from the heat, stir in the fish and season with salt and pepper to taste.

Sprinkle with the cheese and serve immediately. Garnish with lime slices and herbs if liked, and serve rice or new potatoes and a tossed mixed salad as accompaniments.
Serves 4

Creole-style Prawns; Mediterranean Seafood

ASPARAGUS AND FISH SALAD

2 squid
24 mussels
150 ml (¼ pint) dry
    white wine
150 ml (¼ pint) fish
    stock
1 bouquet garni
salt and pepper
12 cooked whole
    prawns
250 g (8 oz) frozen
    asparagus
4 spring onions
2 celery sticks
50 g (2 oz) button
    mushrooms
DRESSING:
1 clove garlic, crushed
2 tablespoons natural
    yogurt
1 tablespoon lemon
    juice
1 tablespoon chopped
    parsley
dash of Tabasco sauce

Prepare the squid (see below) and cut into rings. Place the mussels and squid in a pan and pour over the wine and stock. Add the bouquet garni and salt and pepper to taste. Bring to the boil and simmer for 4 to 5 minutes, until the mussels open. Drain and discard any that have not opened; cool. Discard the shells. Mix in the prawns.

Cook the asparagus in boiling salted water for 5 minutes or until just tender. Drain and cool under running cold water. Drain thoroughly and cut into 5 cm (2 inch) lengths. Chop the spring onions, and thinly slice the celery and mushrooms. Place in a salad bowl with the asparagus and mix well. Stir in the fish.

Mix the dressing ingredients together, seasoning well with salt and pepper, and spoon over the fish and asparagus. Serve immediately, with Gazpacho salad (see page 46).
Serves 4 to 6

CHOOSING FISH

Fresh or smoked, white or oily, flat or shell – there is a vast array of fish ideal to serve as a dinner party main course.

Always check that the fish is very fresh – fresh fish can be recognised by its firm flesh, clear, full and shiny eyes, bright red gills and clean smell.

Don't be put off buying unusual fish because you are not sure how to prepare it – procedures are generally just as simple and certainly as quick as scaling, gutting and filleting of the more popular types.

Mussels should be scrubbed and hair-like beard removed before steaming to open.

To prepare squid, draw back the rim of the body pouch to locate the quill-shaped pen and pull free to discard. Separate the body from the tentacles by pulling gently apart just below the eyes – the inedible head and ink sac will come away together. To skin the body, slip a finger under the skin and peel away gently.

SUMMER GRILLED TROUT

4 trout, cleaned
salt and pepper
1 tablespoon oil
4 spring onions,
    chopped
1 tablespoon chopped
    parsley
juice of ½ lemon
few dill sprigs
TO GARNISH:
dill sprigs
lemon wedges

Season the trout with salt and pepper to taste. Mix together the oil, spring onions, parsley, lemon juice and dill. Divide the mixture into 4 portions and put into the cavities in the trout.

Cook under a preheated medium grill for 5 to 7 minutes on each side, until cooked.

Arrange on a warmed serving dish and serve immediately, garnished with dill and lemon wedges.
Serves 4

Asparagus and Fish Salad; Gazpacho Salad (see page 46)
Summer Grilled Trout

CHICKEN MINCEUR

1 × 1.5 kg (3 lb)
  roasting chicken
  with giblets
finely grated rind and
  juice of 2 limes
2 tarragon sprigs or 2
  teaspoons tarragon
  in vinegar, drained
450 ml (¾ pint) hot
  chicken stock
salt and pepper
TO SERVE:
1 Charentais melon,
  sliced
¼ head of curly
  endive
lime slices

Use the chicken trimmings and giblets to make stock if wished; keep on one side. Truss the chicken (see note on Thanksgiving Turkey, page 36).

Place the lime rind and juice, the tarragon and the simmering stock in a flameproof casserole. Add the chicken, breast side down, cover and simmer for 1¾ to 2 hours, until the juices run clear, turning the chicken halfway through cooking. Cut the chicken into quarters and leave to cool.

Boil the cooking liquid rapidly until reduced by half; leave to cool.

Arrange the melon and endive on a serving dish and lay the chicken on top. Spoon over some of the sauce and hand the rest separately. Garnish with lime slices.
Serves 4

CHICKEN LIVERS IN MARSALA

500 g (1 lb) chicken
  livers
25 g (1 oz) butter
2 onions, chopped
1 clove garlic, crushed
½ teaspoon chilli
  powder
125 g (4 oz) button
  mushrooms, sliced
150 ml (¼ pint)
  Marsala
1 teaspoon dried
  mixed herbs
dash of Worcester-
  shire sauce
salt and pepper
142 ml (5 fl oz)
  double cream
thyme to garnish

Rinse the chicken livers thoroughly and pat dry with kitchen paper. Melt the butter in a pan, add the onions and garlic and fry until lightly browned. Stir in the chilli powder and chicken livers and cook for 5 minutes. Stir in the mushrooms and Marsala. Cook for 5 minutes, then add the herbs, Worcestershire sauce, and salt and pepper to taste. Add the cream, bring to the boil and cook for 2 minutes, stirring until thickened.

Garnish with thyme and serve with rice or pasta, and a green salad.
Serves 6

CHICKEN BREASTS IN VERMOUTH

1 tablespoon oil
1 clove garlic, thinly
  sliced
1 large onion, sliced
6 boneless chicken
  breasts, skinned
salt and pepper
150 ml (¼ pint) dry
  white vermouth
1 tablespoon each
  chopped tarragon
  and parsley
142 ml (5 fl oz)
  double cream
TO GARNISH:
lemon slices
tarragon leaves

Heat the oil in a pan, add the garlic and onion and fry until lightly browned; remove and set aside.

Season the chicken with salt and pepper to taste, add to the pan and brown on both sides. Return the onion and garlic to the pan, increase the heat and add the vermouth and herbs. Cook over high heat for 12 to 15 minutes, turning the chicken twice. Transfer the chicken to a warmed serving dish.

Pour the cream into the pan and cook over high heat, stirring, until the sauce has thickened. Spoon over the chicken and garnish with lemon slices and tarragon to serve.
Serves 6

LEFT: *Chicken Minceur*
OPPOSITE: *Stir-fried Chicken Breasts; Chicken Clamitano*

STIR-FRIED CHICKEN BREASTS

4 chicken breasts
2 tablespoons
  cornflour
2 tablespoons soya
  bean oil
1 teaspoon sesame oil
  (optional)
2 cloves garlic, finely
  chopped
1 × 250 g (8 oz) can
  sliced bamboo
  shoots, drained
150 ml (¼ pint)
  Chinese plum
  sauce
PANCAKES:
25 g (1 oz) plain
  flour
salt
2 eggs, beaten
150 ml (¼ pint)
  water
1 teaspoon brandy
1 tablespoon sesame
  oil
soya bean oil for
  frying
TO GARNISH:
4-8 spring onion fans
cucumber strips

First prepare the pancakes: sift the flour and salt into a bowl. Gradually add the eggs, beating until fairly smooth, then add the water, brandy and sesame oil, if using.

Lightly oil a heavy-based pan and place over high heat until hot. Drop in 3 or 4 tablespoons batter, spacing them well apart, and cook, as separate small pancakes, until golden and bubbly. Turn and cook the other sides until golden. Repeat with the remaining batter. Stack the pancakes on a plate between sheets of greaseproof paper and keep warm over a pan of simmering water.

Skin and bone the chicken breasts and slice diagonally into thin slivers. Coat in the cornflour. Heat the oil(s) in a wok or frying pan, add the chicken in 2 or 3 batches and stir-fry for 3 minutes, pushing the chicken slivers to the side of the pan when cooked. Add the garlic, bamboo shoots and plum sauce. Stir gently and heat through until bubbling.

Transfer the chicken mixture to a warmed serving dish. Garnish with the spring onion fans and cucumber strips, and serve with the pancakes.
Serves 4

CHICKEN CLAMITANO

16 chicken wings
284 ml (10 fl oz) can
  tomato and clam
  juice
3-4 shakes Tabasco
150 ml (¼ pint)
  water
2 bay leaves
12-16 black olives
salt and pepper
parsley to garnish

Put all the ingredients, except salt and pepper, into a pan and simmer, uncovered, for 35 minutes or until the chicken is very tender and the sauce has reduced slightly. Season with salt and pepper to taste, remembering to allow for the saltiness of the olives.

Garnish with parsley and serve with crisply cooked green beans.
Serves 4

DUCK WITH PEPPERCORNS

2 × 1 kg (2 lb)
  oven-ready
  ducklings
salt and pepper
25 g (1 oz) butter
4 shallots, finely
  chopped
150 ml (¼ pint) dry
  white wine
4 tablespoons brandy
4 tablespoons whole
  green peppercorns
  or 1 tablespoon
  black peppercorns,
  coarsely crushed
400 ml (14 fl oz)
  double cream

Prick the skin of the ducklings with a fork and season liberally with salt and pepper. Place in a roasting pan and cook in a preheated moderately hot oven, 200°C (400°F), Gas Mark 6, for about 1¼ hours until tender.

Meanwhile, melt the butter in a pan, add the shallots and cook until transparent. Stir in the wine and brandy, bring to the boil and boil for 5 minutes.

Cut the ducklings into pieces, arrange on a warmed serving dish and keep hot. Add the peppercorns and cream to the sauce and season with salt to taste. Cook for 3 to 5 minutes until thickened.

Spoon the sauce over the ducklings and serve immediately.
Serves 6

STEWED PIGEONS IN WINE

6 rashers streaky
  bacon, derinded
3 young pigeons,
  cleaned
50 g (2 oz) butter
2 tablespoons brandy
150 ml (¼ pint) dry
  white wine
10 pickling onions
6 tablespoons beef
  stock
salt and pepper
125 g (4 oz) button
  mushrooms
1 tablespoon chopped
  parsley
TO GARNISH:
12-16 green olives
thyme sprigs

Wrap 2 rashers bacon around each pigeon and secure with string. Melt the butter in a pan, add the pigeons and cook for 10 minutes until browned all over. Pour over the brandy and wine, bring to the boil and cook for 2 minutes. Add the onions, stock, and salt and pepper to taste. Cover and simmer for 1 hour. Add the mushrooms and parsley and cook for 5 minutes.

Transfer to a warmed serving dish, garnish with olives and thyme; serve immediately.
Serves 6

TURKEY WITH CHESTNUT AND APPLE STUFFING

500 g (1 lb) chestnuts
4 shallots, finely
  chopped
1 tablespoon chopped
  parsley
1 small egg, beaten
salt and pepper
500 g (1 lb) dessert
  apples, peeled,
  cored and chopped
250 g (8 oz) belly
  pork, finely
  chopped
1 × 5.5 kg (12 lb)
  oven-ready turkey
50 g (2 oz) butter
150 ml (¼ pint)
  Madeira
TO GARNISH:
apple rings
watercress sprigs

Cook the chestnuts in boiling water for 15 minutes. Drain, cool, skin and chop. Mix with the shallots, parsley, egg, and salt and pepper to taste.

Place the apples in a pan and cook, stirring, for 5 minutes. Mix into the stuffing, with the pork. Put the stuffing into the neck cavity of the turkey, then sew up the opening.

Place the turkey in a roasting pan, rub the skin with the butter, and season liberally with salt and pepper. Roast in a preheated moderate oven, 180°C (350°F), Gas Mark 4, basting occasionally, for 3½ to 4 hours.

Transfer the turkey to a warmed serving dish. Add the Madeira to the roasting pan, place over high heat and boil for 3 minutes. Spoon over the turkey and serve, garnished with apple rings and watercress.
Serves 10

CHICKEN WITH TARRAGON

25 g (1 oz) butter,
  softened
1 tablespoon chopped
  tarragon
1 clove garlic, crushed
salt and pepper
1 × 1.5 kg (3 lb)
  oven-ready chicken
1 tablespoon olive oil
2 tablespoons brandy
142 ml (5 fl oz)
  double cream
TO GARNISH:
tarragon sprigs
heart-shaped croûtes

Mix together the butter, tarragon, garlic, with salt and pepper to taste, and place inside the chicken. Place, breast side down, in a roasting pan and cook in a preheated moderate oven, 180°C (350°F), Gas Mark 4, for 45 minutes.

Turn the chicken onto its back, baste with the cooking juices, and spoon over the olive oil. Return to the oven for 45 minutes, until tender.

Pour over the brandy and ignite. When the flames have died down, pour over the cream and mix with the juices. Return to the oven for 15 minutes.

Transfer to a warmed serving dish, garnish with tarragon and croûtes and serve immediately.
Serves 4

Duck with Peppercorns; Stewed Pigeons in Wine; Turkey with Chestnut and Apple Stuffing

SOMERSET CHICKEN

1 × 1.5 kg
(3-3½ lb) roasting
chicken
salt and pepper
15 g (½ oz) butter,
softened
150 ml (¼ pint)
cider
NECK STUFFING:
2 rashers smoked
streaky bacon, de-
rinded and chopped
1 small potato, boiled
and mashed
25 g (1 oz) walnuts,
chopped
CAVITY STUFFING:
125 g (4 oz) pork
sausage meat
4 tablespoons
chopped parsley
1 small onion, finely
chopped
125 g (4 oz) pitted
prunes

To prepare the neck stuffing, fry the bacon in its own fat until crisp. Mix together the potato, bacon, bacon fat, nuts, and pepper to taste. Set aside.

To prepare the cavity stuffing, form the sausage meat into walnut-sized balls and roll each in parsley. Push a little onion into each prune.

Sprinkle the chicken cavity with salt and pepper and fill with the sausage meatballs and prunes. Fill the neck cavity with its stuffing. Truss securely (see note, right), spread with the butter and place in a roasting pan.

Cook in a preheated moderately hot oven, 190°C (375°F), Gas Mark 5, for 1¼ hours. Remove chicken and keep warm. Add the cider to the pan and boil rapidly, scraping up all the sediment, until reduced by half.

Carve the chicken and arrange on a warmed serving dish with the stuffing. Hand the sauce separately. Serve with Brussels sprouts.
Serves 4 to 6

THANKSGIVING TURKEY

1 × 5.5-7 kg
(12-16 lb) turkey
with giblets
sea salt
pepper
12-16 button onions
12-16 cloves
125 g (4 oz) unsalted
butter, softened
and diced
150 ml (¼ pint)
water
300 ml (½ pint)
white wine or cider
1 bay leaf
POMEGRANATE
SAUCE:
1 pomegranate
50 g (2 oz) walnuts,
chopped
finely grated rind and
juice of 1 orange
and 1 lemon
4 egg yolks
TO GARNISH:
herb sprigs

Set aside the turkey giblets. Season the cavity of the turkey with the sea salt and pepper. Stud each onion with a clove and use these and half the butter to fill the cavity. Truss the turkey securely (see note) and spread with the remaining butter.

Chop the giblets and place in a roasting pan with the water, wine or cider, and bay leaf. Place the turkey in the pan and cover loosely with foil. Cook in a preheated moderately hot oven, 190°C (375°F), Gas Mark 5, for 15 minutes per pound or until the juices run clear yellow; remove the foil for the last 30 minutes. Transfer to a warmed serving dish and keep warm. Strain the juices and reserve.

To make the pomegranate sauce, cut the pomegranate in half crossways and extract the juice with a lemon squeezer. Add the walnuts, orange and lemon rind and juice, and reserved juices to make up to 600 ml (1 pint). Pour into a pan and simmer gently.

Lightly whisk the egg yolks in a bowl; gradually add 5 to 6 tablespoons of the pomegranate sauce. Remove the pan from the heat, add the egg yolk mixture and whisk well; *do not reheat.*

To serve, garnish the turkey with herbs and surround with sautéed potatoes and buttered carrots. Serve a clove-studded onion with each portion and hand the sauce separately.
Serves 12 to 16
NOTE: To truss a bird, place it back downwards with the centre of the string beneath its tail end. Cross the string over the tail and loop each end around the opposite drumstick, pulling the string to bring the drumsticks over the vent. Turn the bird over. Taking each end of string at a time, loop it around the upper wing, then across the neck flap. Knot the strings at the centre of the back.

Somerset Chicken

CELEBRATION ROAST GOOSE

4.5-5 kg (10-11 lb) goose with giblets
STUFFING:
1 × 435 g (1 lb) can chestnut purée
350 g (12 oz) potatoes, boiled and mashed
8 rashers back bacon, derinded and chopped
1 tablespoon chopped lemon thyme
1 tablespoon chopped sage
finely grated rind of 1 lemon
SAUCE:
25 g (1 oz) butter
1 large onion, chopped
250 g (8 oz) sharp-flavoured dessert apples, peeled, cored and chopped
1 tablespoon clear honey
juice of 1 lemon
½ teaspoon powdered cardamom
salt

Remove the giblets and set aside, chopping the liver. Remove all visible fat from the cavity of the goose and prick the skin of the lower breast and legs well.

Mix the stuffing ingredients together well, adding the chopped goose liver, and pepper to taste. Use to fill the cavity. Truss the goose firmly (see note, opposite), securing the vent with string.

Put the remaining giblets in a roasting pan. Place a rack in the pan and put the goose on top. Pour in 300 ml (½ pint) water.

Cover loosely with foil and cook in a preheated moderately hot oven, 190°C (375°F), Gas Mark 5, for 30 minutes, then lower the temperature to 180°C (350°F), Gas Mark 4. Cook for 3¼ to 3¾ hours, until the juices run clear yellow and a meat thermometer inserted into the leg registers 88°C (190°F); baste occasionally with the liquid and add more water if necessary. Remove the foil after 3 hours to allow the skin to become golden and crisp. Transfer to a warmed serving dish and keep hot.

To make the sauce, melt the butter in a pan and add the onion, apple, honey and lemon juice. Cover and cook for about 12 to 15 minutes, until the onion is soft, then add the cardamom, and salt and pepper to taste. Using a food processor or electric blender, work to a smooth sauce, or rub through a sieve; if a rougher texture is preferred mash with a fork.

Serve the goose accompanied by leek rings and buttered carrot strips. Hand the sauce separately.
Serves 6 to 8

Celebration Roast Goose

SHERRIED TONGUE

1 cured ox tongue,
　about 1.5 kg
　(3½ lb)
1 onion
2 bay leaves
salt and pepper
SAUCE:
40 g (1½ oz) butter
40 g (1½ oz) plain
　flour
150 ml (¼ pint)
　sweet sherry
2 tablespoons
　redcurrant jelly
watercress sprigs to
　garnish

Soak the tongue overnight in cold
water. Drain and put in a large pan,
cover with cold water and bring to
the boil. Boil for 5 minutes, then
drain again. Add fresh cold water to
cover the tongue, the onion, bay
leaves, and salt and pepper to taste.
Bring to the boil and simmer for
2½ to 3 hours, skimming frequently.

Drain, reserving 150 ml (¼ pint)
cooking liquid, and plunge into cold
water. Remove skin and any bones.
Slice the tongue thickly, arrange on a
warmed serving dish and keep warm.

Melt the butter in a pan and stir in
the flour. Gradually stir in the sherry
and reserved cooking liquid. Bring to
the boil and simmer for 5 minutes.
Add the redcurrant jelly and check
the seasoning.

Pour the sauce over the tongue and
serve garnished with watercress.
Serve with Chinese Leaves and Nutty
Potatoes (see page 50).
Serves 6

INVOLTINI WITH TOMATOES

12 thin slices
　Mortadella
12 slices sirloin beef,
　each weighing 50 g
　(2 oz), beaten flat
2 tablespoons oil
1 clove garlic, thinly
　sliced
1 teaspoon dried
　thyme
150 ml (¼ pint) dry
　white wine
1 × 539 g (1 lb 3 oz)
　can tomatoes
1 × 64 g (2¼ oz)
　can tomato purée
1 tablespoon chopped
　basil
salt and pepper
bay or basil leaves to
　garnish

Lay a slice of Mortadella on each beef
slice, roll into a sausage shape and
secure with a cocktail stick. Heat the
oil in a pan, add the meat and brown
on all sides. Drain on kitchen paper.

Pour off the excess fat from the
pan. Add the garlic and thyme, then
stir in the wine and tomatoes, with
their juice. Bring to the boil and boil
rapidly for 10 minutes. Add the
tomato purée and basil. Season to
taste with salt and pepper.

Return the meat rolls to the pan,
cover and cook for 35 to 40 minutes.
Just before serving, increase the heat
to reduce the sauce. Garnish with bay
or basil.

Serve with a green vegetable and
pasta, rice or bread.
Serves 6

*Sherried Tongue; Chinese Leaves (see page 50); Nutty Potatoes
(see page 50)*

VEAL BLANQUETTE

1 kg (2 lb) pie veal,
    cut into 2.5 cm
    (1 inch) cubes
2 onions, chopped
2 carrots, sliced
1 tablespoon lemon
    juice
2 bay leaves
salt and pepper
50 g (2 oz) butter
50 g (2 oz) plain
    flour
3 tablespoons single
    cream
TO GARNISH:
6 rashers streaky
    bacon, derinded
1 lemon, cut into
    wedges
parsley sprigs

Put the veal in a saucepan with the vegetables, lemon juice, bay leaves, and salt and pepper to taste. Add enough water to cover and simmer, covered, for 1½ hours. Remove the meat and vegetables from the pan with a slotted spoon and keep on one side. Discard the bay leaf. Strain the stock, reserving about 600 ml (1 pint).

Melt the butter in the pan and stir in the flour. Gradually add the reserved stock and bring to the boil. Remove from the heat and stir in the cream. Check the seasoning and return the meat and vegetables to the pan. Heat through very gently while preparing the garnish.

Roll up the bacon rashers tightly and thread onto a skewer. Place under a preheated hot grill and cook, turning occasionally, until crisp.

Transfer the veal to a warmed serving dish and garnish with the bacon rolls, lemon wedges and parsley.
Serves 6

PLANNING MENUS

Menu planning can be fun or simply frustrating, especially if you're juggling with personal likes and dislikes. Always plan a menu with variety – a good tip is to follow the seasons. Seasonal dishes offer the virtues of economy, availability and variety in a nutshell.

Variety however, also means differences in colour, texture and flavour. So the old adage of 'wet' food followed by 'dry' food is still a good one to follow. A soup like Mushroom Soup with Madeira (page 23), followed by a crisp main meal such as Lamb Cutlets with Sherry Sauce (page 40), in turn completed with a 'wet' dessert like Zabaione with Macaroons (page 64), would balance nicely.

Alternatively opt for a foreign flavour and choose a menu that reflects the best in a country's cuisine. French cooking is popular and the following menu illustrates the need to balance a rich starter with a light refreshing dessert: Terrine de Canard (page 18); followed by Veal Blanquette (above), Baked Jacket Potatoes (page 52) and Mixed Vegetable Purée (page 50); rounded off with Orange Sorbet (page 56).

STEAKS WITH STILTON

75 g (3 oz) blue
    Stilton cheese
75 g (3 oz) butter,
    softened
1 tablespoon port
1 teaspoon each
    chopped chives and
    thyme.
½ clove garlic,
    crushed
salt and pepper
6 × 2.5 cm (1 inch)
    fillet steaks
thyme sprigs to
    garnish

Put the cheese, butter and port in a blender or food processor and blend until smooth. Stir in the herbs, garlic and salt and pepper to taste. Form the mixture into a roll, wrap in foil and chill in the freezer for 20 minutes.

Season the steaks with salt and pepper and cook under a preheated hot grill for 3 to 5 minutes on each side, according to taste. Arrange on a warmed serving dish.

Cut the butter into 6 and place on the steaks. Garnish with thyme and serve immediately, with courgettes.
Serves 6

Baked Jacket Potatoes (see page 52); Mixed Vegetable Purée (see page 50); Veal Blanquette

BEEF STROGANOFF

25 g (1 oz) butter
2 onions, sliced
1-2 cloves garlic,
 crushed
750 g (1½ lb) rump
 or sirloin steak
2 tablespoons dry red
 wine
125 g (4 oz) button
 mushrooms, sliced
1 teaspoon French
 mustard
150 g (5.2 oz)
 natural yogurt
salt and pepper
1 tablespoon each
 chopped thyme and
 parsley
croûtons of fried bread
 to serve

Melt the butter in a large frying pan, add the onions and garlic and fry until lightly browned. Cut the steak into thin strips, add to the pan and brown on all sides. Add the wine and boil for 5 minutes, until the liquid has reduced. Add the mushrooms, mustard, yogurt, and salt and pepper to taste and simmer for 5 minutes.

Just before serving, stir in the herbs. Garnish with croûtons and serve with noodles.

Serves 4

NOTE: This is an ideal dish to serve if you are concerned with calories. For a richer dish, substitute 142 ml (5 fl oz) soured cream for the yogurt.

Beef Stroganoff; Lamb Cutlets with Sherry Sauce

LAMB CUTLETS WITH SHERRY SAUCE

8 lamb cutlets
1 clove garlic, sliced
1 egg, beaten
50 g (2 oz) white
 breadcrumbs
1-2 tablespoons oil
25 g (1 oz) unsalted
 butter
1 tablespoon each
 chopped thyme,
 parsley, sage and
 chives
150 ml (¼ pint) dry
 sherry
142 ml (5 fl oz)
 double cream
salt and pepper
TO GARNISH:
125 g (4 oz) green
 olives
sage leaves

Cut small slits in the cutlets and push in the slivered garlic. Coat each cutlet with egg and breadcrumbs, then chill for 20 minutes.

Heat the oil and butter in a frying pan, add the cutlets and brown on both sides. Lower the heat and cook for 6 minutes on each side. Drain on kitchen paper and arrange on a warmed serving dish; keep warm.

Add the herbs and sherry to the pan and boil rapidly for 2 minutes, until thickened. Stir in the cream, and salt and pepper to taste.

Spoon over the cutlets and serve immediately, garnished with the olives and sage.

Serves 4

LAMB KEBABS

2 × 150 g (5.2 oz) cartons natural yogurt
1 tablespoon ground coriander seeds
½ teaspoon chilli powder
1 tablespoon oil
salt
750 g (1½ lb) boned leg of lamb, cubed
4 onions
2 red peppers, cored and seeded
8 tomatoes
2 tablespoons finely chopped coriander

Put the yogurt, coriander seeds, chilli, oil, and salt to taste in a large bowl and stir to combine. Add the meat, mix well, cover and leave in the refrigerator overnight.

Cut the onions in quarters and separate the layers. Cut the peppers into squares and the tomatoes in half.

Thread the onion, lamb and red pepper alternately on 8 skewers, beginning and ending each kebab with a tomato half. Cook under a preheated hot grill for about 10 minutes, turning frequently and basting with any remaining marinade as necessary. Sprinkle with the chopped coriander to serve.
Serves 4

COCONUT LAMB CURRY

grated flesh of ½ fresh coconut
4 dried red chillis
1 teaspoon cumin seeds
1 tablespoon each coriander seeds and poppy seeds
1 teaspoon peppercorns
2.5 cm (½ inch) piece ginger, chopped
2 cloves garlic
1 teaspoon turmeric
2 tablespoons lemon juice
4 tablespoons oil
2 onions, chopped
750 g (1½ lb) boned leg of lamb, cubed
1 × 227 g (8 oz) can tomatoes
salt
2 tablespoons finely chopped coriander

Heat the coconut, chillies, cumin, coriander and poppy seeds in a dry frying pan for about 1 minute. Place in an electric blender or food processor with the peppercorns, ginger, garlic, turmeric and lemon juice and blend to a paste.

Heat the oil in a pan, add the onions and fry until soft, then add the prepared paste and fry for 5 minutes. Add the lamb and cook, stirring, for 5 minutes, then add the tomatoes with their juice and salt to taste. Bring to simmering point, cover and cook for about 1 hour, until tender.

Sprinkle with chopped coriander to serve.
Serves 4
NOTE: If fresh coconut is not available, blend the other spices and lemon juice as above and add 50 g (2 oz) creamed coconut to the onions with the blended spices.

Lamb Kebabs; Coconut Lamb Curry

VEAL SCALOPPINE WITH TOMATOES

2 tablespoons oil
2 cloves garlic, thinly
   sliced
500 g (1 lb) veal
   escalope, very
   thinly sliced and
   pounded flat
salt and pepper
250 ml (8 fl oz) dry
   white wine
500 g (1 lb)
   tomatoes, skinned,
   seeded and chopped
dash of Worcester-
   shire sauce
1 tablespoon tomato
   purée
1 teaspoon each dried
   oregano and
   marjoram

Heat the oil in a pan, add the garlic and cook for 1 minute. Season the veal with salt and pepper to taste, add to the pan and brown quickly on both sides.

Pour off any oil. Add the wine and tomatoes to the pan, bring to the boil and boil rapidly for 10 minutes, until the sauce has thickened. Stir in the Worcestershire sauce, tomato purée and herbs and cook for 5 minutes.

Transfer to a warmed serving dish and serve immediately.
Serves 4

ITALIAN VEAL ROLLS

6 thin slices ham
6 veal escalopes, each
   weighing 50 g
   (2 oz), beaten flat
50 g (2 oz) pork fat,
   finely chopped
1 clove garlic, sliced
2 tablespoons pine nuts
2 tablespoons
   sultanas
2 tablespoons grated
   Parmesan cheese
3 tablespoons
   chopped parsley
6 slices Gruyère
   cheese
salt and pepper
1 tablespoon oil
300 ml (½ pint) dry
   white wine
1 tablespoon tomato
   purée

Lay a slice of ham on each escalope. Sprinkle with the pork fat, garlic, pine nuts, sultanas, Parmesan cheese and 1 tablespoon of the parsley. Top with the Gruyère cheese and season well with salt and pepper. Roll up and secure with cocktail sticks.

Heat the oil in a pan, add the veal rolls and brown on all sides. Pour over the wine, season well and bring to the boil. Cover and simmer for 25 to 30 minutes, until tender. Remove the rolls from the pan with a slotted spoon and arrange on a warmed serving dish. Keep warm.

Boil the liquid in the pan until reduced by half, then stir in the tomato purée and remaining parsley. Spoon the sauce over the veal rolls.

Serve with rice and a tossed green salad.
Serves 6

PORK STUFFED WITH PÂTÉ

2 pork tenderloins
125 g (4 oz) smooth
    pâté
salt and pepper
25 g (1 oz) unsalted
    butter
1 clove garlic, crushed
50 g (2 oz)
    mushrooms,
    chopped
150 ml (¼ pint) dry
    sherry
150 ml (¼ pint) dry
    white wine
1 teaspoon French
    mustard
dash of
    Worcestershire
    sauce
½ teaspoon mixed
    herbs
2 tablespoons double
    cream
2 tablespoons
    chopped chives
1 tablespoon capers
    (optional)

Using a sharp knife, make a horizontal cut through the centre of the pork, taking care not to cut right through. Spread the pâté over the cut surface and sew up, ensuring that the pâté is enclosed. Season with salt and pepper.

Melt the butter in a large frying pan, add the meat and brown on all sides. Remove from the pan.

Add the garlic to the pan and fry until browned. Add the mushrooms and cook for 1 minute. Add the sherry, wine, mustard, Worcestershire sauce and herbs. Bring to the boil, return the pork to the pan, cover and simmer for 35 to 40 minutes, turning occasionally. Remove the pork from the pan; keep warm.

Increase the heat and boil the liquid in the pan until thickened. Stir in the cream, cook for 2 minutes.

Slice the pork and arrange on a warmed serving dish. Add the chives and capers, if using, to the sauce. Spoon over the pork and serve immediately, with a green vegetable.
Serves 4 to 6

SKEWERED SICILIAN PORK

750 g (1½ lb) pork
    fillet
4 × 2.5 cm (1 inch)
    slices French
    bread, quartered
8 small slices Parma
    ham or streaky
    bacon rashers,
    halved and rolled
    up
sage and bay leaves
MARINADE:
4 tablespoons olive
    oil
2 tablespoons lemon
    juice
1 clove garlic, crushed
1 tablespoon mixed
    herbs
salt and pepper

Cut the pork into 2.5 cm (1 inch) cubes.

Put the marinade ingredients in a bowl, with salt and pepper to taste, and mix well. Add the pork cubes and marinate for 1 to 2 hours, turning occasionally. Remove the meat from the marinade with a slotted spoon; reserve the marinade.

Arrange the pork, French bread and Parma ham or bacon alternately on 8 skewers, interspersing with sage and bay leaves to taste.

Cook under a preheated moderate grill, or over a charcoal grill, for 10 minutes on each side, until the pork is tender and browned, basting with the remaining marinade during cooking.

Serve hot, with vegetables.
Serves 4 to 6

ENTERTAINING ITALIAN-STYLE

The Italians love their food and illustrate such devotion with their mouth-watering acclaimed specialities like pasta, pizza, Mediterranean fish dishes, and, of course, ice cream.

Choose an Italian menu when you are confident that your guests will enjoy such hot-blooded fare – for Italian cooking is never short on flavour.

Start with Prosciutto con Fichi (page 11) – paper-thin slices of Parma ham, served with ripe succulent melon wedges and decorative ripe fig 'flowers'. Follow with a rich aromatic dish of Italian Veal Rolls (page 42) – veal escalopes stuffed with ham, garlic, pine nuts, sultanas and Parmesan cheese, then cooked in wine. Accompany with Tagliatelle Pesto (page 12) and a green salad. Crown the meal with Zucotto (page 61), a rich sponge and cream concoction. Serve with classic Italian wines like Barolo, Soave, Verdicchio or Orvieto.

OPPOSITE: *Tagliatelle Pesto (see page 12); Italian Veal Rolls*
RIGHT: *Skewered Sicilian Pork*

SPINACH AND CHEESE PANCAKES

PANCAKE BATTER:
*scant 125 g (4 oz)
   plain flour*
¼ teaspoon salt
2 small eggs
1 tablespoon oil
*150 ml (¼ pint)
   milk*
6 tablespoons water
FILLING:
*250 g (8 oz) frozen
   chopped spinach,
   cooked*
*250 g (8 oz) Ricotta
   or curd cheese*
*25 g (1 oz) grated
   Parmesan cheese*
1 egg, beaten
grated nutmeg
salt and pepper
TOPPING:
25 g (1 oz) butter
*3 tablespoons grated
   Parmesan cheese*
*5 tablespoons chicken
   stock*

Sift the flour and salt into a bowl. Make a well in the centre and add the eggs, oil and milk. Beat until smooth, then stir in the water. Cover and chill for 1 to 2 hours.

Lightly oil an 18 cm (7 inch) frying pan and place over moderate heat. When hot, pour in just enough batter to cover the base. When the pancake is set and the underside lightly browned, turn and briefly cook the other side. Repeat with the remaining batter, making 8 pancakes.

Squeeze the spinach dry, then mix the filling ingredients together, seasoning liberally with nutmeg, salt and pepper. Divide between the pancakes, roll up loosely and arrange in a buttered ovenproof dish. Dot with the butter, sprinkle with the Parmesan cheese and pour in the stock.

Bake in a preheated moderately hot oven, 200°C (400°F), Gas Mark 6, for about 20 minutes until golden. Serve immediately.
Serves 4

Spinach and Cheese Pancakes

COURGETTE SOUFFLÉ

2 tablespoons oil
*750 g (1½ lb)
   courgettes, grated*
*50 g (2 oz)
   margarine or butter*
*50 g (2 oz)
   wholemeal flour*
200 ml (8 fl oz) milk
3 eggs, separated
salt and pepper
grated nutmeg
TOMATO SAUCE
(optional):
*25 g (1 oz)
   margarine or butter*
*500 g (1 lb)
   tomatoes, skinned
   and chopped*
*1 tablespoon chopped
   parsley*
*1 tablespoon chopped
   chives*

Heat the oil in a large pan, add the courgettes and cook gently for 10 minutes, stirring occasionally.

Melt the fat in another pan, remove from the heat and stir in the flour. Add the milk and mix well. Return to the heat and bring to the boil, stirring; simmer for 3 minutes. Cool slightly then add the egg yolks, courgettes, and salt, pepper and nutmeg to taste.

Whisk the egg whites until stiff and carefully fold into the mixture. Turn into a greased 1.2 litre (2 pint) ovenproof dish and place in a roasting pan containing 2.5 cm (1 inch) water. Cook in a preheated moderately hot oven, 190°C (375°F), Gas Mark 5, for 55 minutes to 1 hour.

Meanwhile, make the tomato sauce if using. Melt the fat in a pan and add the tomatoes, herbs, and salt and pepper to taste. Cook gently for 5 to 10 minutes. Sieve, or work in an electric blender until smooth; strain.

Serve immediately, as a main dish or starter, with the sauce, if liked.
Serves 4 to 6

VEGETARIAN MENUS

A vegetarian dinner party menu fills most people with fear – yet doesn't seem quite so daunting if treated as a menu without meat. Consider it as such and there are a vast range of tasty, colourful and, moreover, interesting dishes from which to choose to make a flavoursome menu.

For starters, consider Marinated Mushrooms (page 10), Guacamole (page 11), Mixed Vegetable Salad (page 13) or Melon, Tomato and Kiwi Vinaigrette (page 14).

Main courses often prove more difficult but there is still a good choice: Spinach and Cheese Pancakes (above), Courgette Soufflé (above), Cheesy Courgettes (page 45) or a taste of the orient with Indian Vegetable Curry (page 45). Desserts are rarely a problem, unless you are catering for a strict vegetarian who does not eat dairy produce.

A good well-balanced vegetarian menu would be: Sweet Pepper Soup (page 26); followed by a main course of Spinach Roulade (page 45), Nutty Potatoes (page 50) and Tomato and Leek Salad (page 47); finished with a Hazelnut Shortcake (page 61) served with natural yogurt.

SPINACH ROULADE

500 g (1 lb) spinach
4 eggs, separated
salt and pepper
grated nutmeg
FILLING:
3 tablespoons oil
1 onion, chopped
250 g (8 oz)
  mushrooms, sliced
1 tablespoon
  wholemeal flour
150 ml (¼ pint)
  milk
1 tablespoon grated
  Parmesan cheese

Cook the spinach in a large pan with just the water clinging to the leaves after washing, for 5 minutes. Drain thoroughly and chop finely.

Place in a bowl with the egg yolks, and salt, pepper and nutmeg to taste; mix well. Whisk the egg whites until stiff and fold into the mixture.

Spread the mixture evenly in a lined and greased 30 × 20 cm (12 × 8 inch) Swiss roll tin. Cook in a preheated moderately hot oven, 200°C (400°F), Gas Mark 6, for 10 to 15 minutes until risen and firm.

Heat the oil in a pan, add the onion and fry until soft. Add the mushrooms and fry for 2 to 3 minutes. Stir in the flour, then gradually stir in the milk. Add salt and pepper to taste and simmer for 2 to 3 minutes.

Sprinkle the cheese over a sheet of greaseproof paper. Turn the roulade out onto the paper and peel off the lining paper. Spread with the filling and roll up. Serve immediately, with any extra mushroom sauce handed separately.
Serves 4

Indian Vegetable Curry

CHEESY COURGETTES

6 plump courgettes,
  about 13 cm
  (5 inches) long
salt and pepper
25 g (1 oz) white
  bread, crusts
  removed, soaked in
  2 tablespoons milk
125 g (4 oz) Ricotta
  or curd cheese
1 clove garlic, crushed
¼ teaspoon dried
  oregano
40 g (1½ oz) grated
  Parmesan cheese
1 egg yolk

Parboil the courgettes in boiling salted water for 5 minutes; drain. Halve lengthways and scoop out the centres; chop finely. Reserve the shells.

Squeeze the bread dry, reserving the liquid, and mix with the chopped courgette and remaining ingredients; add a little of the liquid if necessary to give a spreading consistency. Add salt and pepper to taste.

Fill the courgette shells with the mixture and arrange in a well oiled shallow baking dish. Cook in a preheated moderately hot oven, 190°C (375°F), Gas Mark 5, for 35 to 40 minutes, until tender and golden.
Serves 6

INDIAN VEGETABLE CURRY

3 tablespoons oil
1 teaspoon fennel
  seeds
2 onions, sliced
1 teaspoon chilli
  powder
1 tablespoon ground
  coriander seeds
2.5 cm (1 inch) piece
  ginger, chopped
2 aubergines, sliced
175 g (6 oz) shelled
  peas
125 g (4 oz)
  potatoes, cubed
1 × 227 g (8 oz) can
  tomatoes

Heat the oil in a large pan, add the fennel seeds and fry for a few seconds, then add the onions and fry until soft and golden. Add the chilli powder, coriander, ginger and salt to taste and fry for 2 minutes. Add the aubergines, peas and potatoes and cook for 5 minutes, stirring occasionally.

Add the tomatoes with their juice, cover and simmer for 30 minutes, or until the peas are tender and the sauce is thick.
Serves 4
NOTE: See page 52 for accompaniment ideas, and page 66 for Shrikand, a traditional Indian dessert.

GAZPACHO SALAD

*1 each green, red and
   yellow pepper
4 large tomatoes
1 small cucumber
1 medium Spanish
   onion
4 tablespoons
   chopped parsley*
DRESSING:
*4 tablespoons olive
   oil
2 tablespoons wine
   vinegar
2 cloves garlic,
   crushed
pinch of ground
   cumin
1 teaspoon clear
   honey
2 spring onions,
   chopped
salt and pepper*
TO GARNISH:
few black olives

Remove the core and seeds from the
peppers and thinly slice them;
roughly chop the tomatoes. Remove
the seeds from the cucumber and
chop. Finely chop the onion.

   Layer the pepper, tomatoes,
cucumber and onion in a glass bowl.
Sprinkle the parsley liberally over
each layer.

   Mix all the dressing ingredients
together, with salt and pepper to
taste, and pour over the salad. Cover
and leave to stand for 15 minutes
before serving. Arrange the black
olives on top to serve.
Serves 4
(Illustrated on page 31)

CHINESE SALAD

*2.5 cm (1 inch) piece
   root ginger, finely
   chopped
4 tablespoons French
   dressing (see page
   151)
1 Chinese cabbage
½ cucumber
125 g (4 oz)
   beanshoots
6 spring onions,
   chopped
1 tablespoon chopped
   parsley, to garnish*

Mix the ginger with the dressing and
leave for 30 minutes. Shred the
Chinese cabbage and cut the
cucumber into julienne strips. Place
all the ingredients in a bowl and toss
thoroughly to combine with the
dressing. Transfer to a serving dish
and sprinkle with the parsley.
Serves 6

RED CABBAGE
AND APPLE SALAD

*350 g (12 oz) red
   cabbage
1 small leek
6 tablespoons
   Vinaigrette
   dressing (see page
   153)
3 dessert apples,
   quartered and cored*

Finely shred the cabbage, and thinly
slice the leek. Place in a salad bowl,
add the dressing and toss thoroughly.
Leave to marinate for 1 hour, tossing
occasionally.

   Slice the apples thinly. Add to the
bowl and toss again just before
serving.
Serves 8

ARTICHOKES
WITH TOMATOES

*1 kg (2 lb) Jerusalem
   artichokes
salt and pepper
3 tablespoons olive
   oil
4 tomatoes, skinned
   and chopped
1 teaspoon chopped
   marjoram*

Simmer the artichokes in boiling
salted water for 20 minutes until
almost cooked. Drain and cut into
even-sized pieces.

   Heat the oil in a pan, add the
tomatoes, marjoram, artichokes, and
salt and pepper to taste. Cover and
simmer for 5 to 10 minutes. Transfer
to a warmed dish. Serve immediately.
Serves 4

Chinese Salad; Red Cabbage and Apple Salad

TOMATO AND BASIL SALAD

The piquant flavour of basil greatly enhances the flavour of the tomatoes, and the mellowness of the olive oil brings out the full flavour of this delicious salad. Serve as a tasty main course accompaniment or a refreshing summer first course.

500 g (1 lb) Marmande tomatoes
salt and pepper
3 tablespoons olive oil
2 tablespoons chopped basil

Slice the tomatoes thinly and lay them in a shallow serving dish, sprinkling each layer with salt and pepper. Pour over the oil and sprinkle with the basil.
Serves 4

NOTE: Marmande tomatoes are the large round variety, often called Mediterranean tomatoes.

CUCUMBER WITH MINT

The refreshing quality of this salad makes it especially suitable to serve with curries. It is also very pleasant served on its own after a fish course.

1 cucumber, thinly sliced
salt
1 bunch of mint, finely chopped
8 tablespoons Yogurt dressing (page 152)

Place the cucumber in a colander, sprinkle with salt and leave to drain for 30 minutes. Dry the cucumber on kitchen paper and place in a shallow serving dish. Add the mint and dressing and mix well.
Serves 4 to 6

TOMATO AND LEEK SALAD

500 g (1 lb) tomatoes, sliced
125 g (4 oz) leeks, thinly sliced
4 tablespoons Honey and lemon dressing (see page 151)
1 tablespoon chopped parsley

Arrange the tomatoes and leeks in layers in a shallow serving dish, finishing with leeks. Pour over the dressing and sprinkle with the parsley.
Serves 4

NOTE: The leeks may be marinated in the dressing for 15 minutes before combining with the tomatoes if a more mellow flavour is preferred.

Tomato and Basil Salad; Cucumber with Mint; Tomato and Leek Salad

MIXED BEAN SALAD

125 g (4 oz) butter
  beans
125 g (4 oz) red
  kidney beans
125 g (4 oz) haricot
  beans
salt
125 g (4 oz) French
  beans, cut into
  2.5 cm (1 inch)
  lengths
6 spring onions,
  chopped
4 tablespoons French
  dressing (see page
  151)
2 tablespoons
  chopped parsley

Soak the beans separately overnight.
Drain and place in separate pans.
Cover with cold water, bring to the
boil and boil steadily for 15 minutes.
Lower the heat, cover and simmer for
1 to 1½ hours, adding a little salt
towards the end of cooking; drain.

Cook the French beans in boiling
salted water for 7 to 8 minutes; drain.
Place all the beans in a bowl and mix
in the onions and dressing while still
warm. Leave to cool.

Stir in the parsley and transfer to a
salad bowl to serve.
Serves 6 to 8

COLESLAW WITH YOGURT DRESSING

½ medium white
  cabbage, finely
  shredded
2 celery sticks, chopped
2 dessert apples, cored
  and chopped
1 small onion, finely
  chopped
50 g (2 oz) sultanas
50 g (2 oz) walnuts,
  chopped
2 tablespoons chopped
  parsley (optional)
120 ml (4 fl oz)
  Yogurt dressing
  (see page 152)

Place all the ingredients in a salad
bowl and toss thoroughly to serve.
Serves 6

*Swedish Potato Salad; Potato and Radish Vinaigrette;
Mixed Bean Salad*

SWEDISH POTATO SALAD

750 g (1½ lb) small new potatoes
salt
2 tablespoons French dressing (page 151)
125 g (4 oz) cooked beetroot, diced
1 pickled dill cucumber, diced
5 tablespoons Yogurt dressing (page 152)
1 tablespoon chopped dill

Scrub the potatoes clean but leave the skins on. Cook in boiling salted water until tender. Drain and mix with the French dressing while still warm. Leave to cool.

Add the beetroot, cucumber and yogurt dressing. Mix well, then transfer to a salad bowl. Sprinkle with the dill to serve.
Serves 6

POTATO AND RADISH VINAIGRETTE

500 g (1 lb) small new potatoes
salt
4 tablespoons Vinaigrette dressing (see page 153)
4 spring onions, sliced
1 bunch of radishes, thinly sliced

Scrub the potatoes clean but leave the skins on. Cook in boiling salted water until tender. Drain well and mix with the dressing while still warm. Leave to cool.

Add the spring onions and radishes, mix well and transfer to a salad bowl to serve.
Serves 4

BROWN RICE SALAD

250 g (8 oz) brown rice
salt
3 spring onions, finely chopped
1 red pepper, cored and seeded
50 g (2 oz) raisins
50 g (2 oz) cashew nuts, roasted
2 tablespoons chopped parsley (optional)
6 tablespoons Soy sauce dressing (see page 153)

Cook the rice in boiling salted water for 40 to 45 minutes until tender. Rinse, drain well and cool.

Place the rice in a bowl. Add the remaining ingredients and toss thoroughly just before serving.
Serves 6

COURGETTE AND TOMATO SALAD

250 g (8 oz) courgettes, very thinly sliced (see note)
6 tablespoons Garlic dressing (see page 151)
6 small tomatoes, sliced
50 g (2 oz) black olives, halved and stoned
1 tablespoon chopped marjoram
1 tablespoon chopped parsley

Place the courgettes in a bowl, pour over the dressing and leave to marinate overnight.

Add the remaining ingredients, toss thoroughly and turn into a salad bowl.
Serves 4 to 6
NOTE: The very small, young courgettes are the most suitable to use raw in salads. They must be sliced very thinly to allow the flavour of the dressing to be absorbed.

Courgette and Tomato Salad

RATATOUILLE

3 tablespoons olive
　oil
2 onions, sliced
2 cloves garlic, crushed
1 aubergine, sliced
1 green pepper, cored,
　seeded and sliced
250 g (8 oz)
　courgettes, sliced
250 g (8 oz)
　tomatoes, skinned
　and sliced
salt and pepper

Heat the oil in a flameproof casserole, add the onion and garlic and fry gently until translucent. Add the aubergine and fry for 5 minutes, turning frequently. Add the remaining ingredients, seasoning liberally with salt and pepper. Stir well. Cover and cook in a preheated moderate oven, 180°C (350°F), Gas Mark 4, for 1 hour. Serve hot.
Serves 6
NOTE: This can also be served cold as a starter.

MIXED VEGETABLE PURÉE

500 g (1 lb) parsnips
500 g (1 lb) carrots
500 g (1 lb) Brussels
　sprouts
salt and pepper
142 ml (5 fl oz)
　double cream
75 g (3 oz) butter
parsley sprigs to
　garnish

Cut the parsnips and carrots into even-sized pieces. Cook the parsnips, carrots and sprouts separately in boiling salted water: parsnips for 20 minutes, carrots for 15 minutes and sprouts for 8 minutes. Drain.
　Sieve or blend each vegetable separately with one-third of the cream and one-third of the butter. Season liberally with salt and pepper.
　To serve, arrange in stripes in an oblong dish or in sections in a round dish. Garnish with parsley.
Serves 6
(Illustrated on page 39)

FRENCH-STYLE PEAS

4 lettuce leaves
½ bunch spring onions
750 g (1½ lb) frozen
　peas
150 ml (¼ pint) water
1 teaspoon lemon
　juice
1 teaspoon sugar
50 g (2 oz) butter

Shred the lettuce and slice the spring onions. Put all the ingredients, except the butter, in a saucepan. Bring to the boil, cover and simmer for 8 minutes; drain.
　Place in a warmed serving dish, dot with the butter and serve.
Serves 6

CHINESE LEAVES

1 head of Chinese
　leaves, shredded
salt
50 g (2 oz) butter
grated rind and juice
　of 1 orange
½ teaspoon grated
　nutmeg
chopped parsley to
　garnish

Cook the Chinese leaves in a little boiling salted water for 5 minutes. Drain well.
　Put the butter, orange rind and juice, and nutmeg in the pan. Add the Chinese leaves and toss well.
　Transfer to a warmed serving dish and serve hot, garnished with parsley.
Serves 6
(Illustrated on page 38)

NUTTY POTATOES

1 kg (2 lb) potatoes,
　boiled
50 g (2 oz) butter
2 tablespoons milk
125 g (4 oz) chopped
　mixed nuts

Mash the potatoes with the butter and milk; leave to cool. Shape into a roll and cut into 24 pieces. Using your hands, roll into balls then flatten into cakes. Coat with chopped nuts.
　Place on a greased baking sheet and cook in a preheated moderate oven, 180°C (350°F), Gas Mark 4, for 20 minutes, until crisp and golden.
Serves 6
(Illustrated on page 38)

French-style Peas; Ratatouille

POTATOES WITH CHEESE AND BACON

2 tablespoons olive oil
75 g (3 oz) streaky bacon, derinded and chopped
1 kg (2 lb) potatoes, thinly sliced
150 g (5 oz) Gruyère cheese, grated
salt and pepper
3 cloves garlic, crushed
2 tablespoons chopped parsley
4 tablespoons double cream

Heat the oil in a heavy-based pan, add the bacon and fry until golden and crisp.

Arrange the potatoes, cheese and bacon in layers in a greased ovenproof dish, seasoning each layer with salt and pepper to taste. Sprinkle the top with garlic and parsley.

Cover and cook in a preheated moderately hot oven, 190°C (375°F), Gas Mark 5, for 45 to 50 minutes. Pour over the cream, cover and return to the oven for 5 minutes. Serve immediately.
Serves 4 to 6

MEDITERRANEAN POTATO DISH

This dish is delicious with roast or cold meats.

1/2 head garlic cloves, unpeeled
1 bouquet garni
300 ml (1/2 pint) water
8 potatoes, thickly sliced
4 large tomatoes, skinned, seeded and sliced
salt and pepper
chopped parsley to garnish

Place the garlic, bouquet garni and water in a pan and simmer for 20 to 30 minutes. Cool, remove both from the pan, discard the bouquet garni and peel the garlic. Pound the garlic in a mortar with the water from the pan until smooth.

Spoon half the garlic residue into a small ovenproof dish. Arrange the potatoes and tomatoes in layers on top and season well with salt and pepper. Spoon over the remaining garlic residue.

Cover and cook in a preheated moderate oven, 180°C (350°F), Gas Mark 4, for 1 to 1¼ hours, until the potatoes are tender. Serve garnished with parsley.
Serves 4 to 6

Potatoes with Cheese and Bacon; Potatoes Lyonnaise; Mediterranean Potato Dish

POTATOES LYONNAISE

40 g (1½ oz) butter
500 g (1 lb) onions, finely sliced
1 kg (2 lb) potatoes, finely sliced
salt and pepper
2 tablespoons chopped parsley

Melt the butter in a pan, add the onions and fry until golden.

Arrange the potatoes and onions in layers in an ovenproof dish; sprinkle each layer liberally with salt and pepper and the parsley. Cover and cook in a preheated moderate oven, 180°C (350°F), Gas Mark 4, for 1 to 1¼ hours until the potatoes are tender. Serve hot.
Serves 4 to 6

CHAPATIS

250 g (8 oz)
  wholemeal flour
1 teaspoon salt
200 ml (1/3 pint)
  water
  (approximately)

Place the flour and salt in a bowl. Make a well in the centre, gradually stir in the water and work to a soft supple dough. Knead for 10 minutes, then cover and leave in a cool place for 30 minutes. Knead again very thoroughly, then divide into 12 pieces. Roll out each piece on a floured surface into a thin round pancake.

Lightly grease a griddle or heavy-based frying pan with a little ghee or oil and place over a moderate heat. Add a chapati and cook until blisters appear. Press down with a fish slice, then turn and cook the other side until lightly coloured. Remove from the pan and keep warm while cooking the rest.

Brush a little butter on one side and serve warm, with curries (see page 41 and 45).
Makes 12

MUSHROOM AND ONION CASSEROLE

50 g (2 oz) butter
500 g (1 lb) onions,
  roughly chopped
500 g (1 lb)
  mushrooms, sliced
200 ml (1/3 pint) stock
2 tablespoons sherry
2 tablespoons lemon
  juice
salt and pepper
chopped parsley to
  garnish

Melt the butter in a flameproof casserole. Add the onions and fry gently for 10 minutes, until soft. Add the mushrooms, stock, sherry, lemon juice, and salt and pepper to taste.

Cover and cook in a preheated moderate oven, 180°C (350°F), Gas Mark 4, for 15 minutes. Serve hot, garnished with parsley.
Serves 4

TOMATO RICE

250 g (8 oz) long-
  grain rice
3 tablespoons oil
1 onion, sliced
1 clove garlic, crushed
2.5 cm (1 inch) piece
  ginger, chopped
1 × 539 g (1 lb 3 oz)
  can tomatoes
salt
2 tablespoons finely
  chopped coriander

Wash the rice under running cold water, then soak in fresh cold water for 30 minutes; drain thoroughly.

Heat the oil in a large pan, add the onion and fry until golden. Add the garlic and ginger and fry for 2 minutes. Add the rice, stir well and fry for 2 minutes.

Break up the tomatoes in their juice and add to the rice with salt to taste. Bring to the boil, cover and simmer for 15 to 20 minutes until tender.

Transfer to a warmed serving dish and sprinkle with the coriander.
Serves 4

INDIAN CAULIFLOWER

3 tablespoons oil
1 onion, sliced
1/2 teaspoon turmeric
1 cauliflower, broken
  into florets
salt
2 green chillies,
  seeded
1 green, 1 yellow and
  1 red pepper,
  cored, seeded and
  cut into strips

Heat the oil in a pan, add the onion and fry until soft. Add the turmeric and cook for 1 minute. Add the cauliflower and salt to taste, stir well, cover and cook gently for about 10 minutes, until the cauliflower is almost cooked.

Add the chillies and peppers, stir and cook for a further 5 minutes or until tender. Serve as an accompaniment to curries.
Serves 4

BAKED JACKET POTATOES

6 potatoes, each
  weighing about
  250 g (8 oz)
75 g (3 oz) butter
salt and pepper
chopped parsley to
  garnish

Scrub the potatoes well and dry. Cut a cross on one side of each. Rub all over with butter paper and cook on the rack in a preheated moderately hot oven, 200°C (400°F), Gas Mark 6, for 1¼ hours. Push back the skin to open up the cross and top with the butter. Sprinkle with salt and pepper and chopped parsley to serve.
Serves 6

MIXED STIR-FRY

1 onion
2.5 cm (1 inch) piece
  fresh root ginger,
  peeled
2 cloves garlic, crushed
175 g (6 oz) carrots
4 celery sticks
175 g (6 oz) white
  cabbage
4 tablespoons
  sunflower oil
125 g (4 oz) bean
  sprouts
2 teaspoons soy sauce
2 teaspoons vinegar
1 teaspoon caster
  sugar
salt and pepper

Chop the onion and root ginger finely. Transfer to a bowl and combine with the garlic.

Finely slice the carrots and celery; shred the cabbage.

Heat the oil in a large frying pan or wok and add the onion mixture. Stir-fry for 1 minute.

Add the carrots and stir-fry for a further minute. Add the remaining vegetables and stir-fry for 3 minutes.

Sprinkle with the soy sauce, vinegar and sugar, season well with salt and pepper and stir together for 1 minute. Serve immediately.
Serves 6

AUBERGINE FRITTERS

3 aubergines
1 tablespoon salt
125 g (4 oz) plain
  flour
1 egg
150 ml (¼ pint)
  milk
1 teaspoon garam
  masala
oil for deep-frying

Slice the aubergines. Sprinkle with the salt and leave to drain for 30 minutes.

Place the flour, egg, milk and garam masala in an electric blender or food processor and work to a smooth batter.

Rinse the aubergine slices and pat dry with kitchen paper. Coat each slice in the prepared batter and deep-fry for 8 to 10 minutes, until crisp and golden. Drain on kitchen paper and serve immediately.
Serves 4

RUMBLEDETHUMPS

A traditional Scottish dish which makes an interesting vegetable accompaniment.

500 g (1 lb) cabbage
salt
1 onion
750 g (1½ lb)
  potatoes, boiled
  and mashed
125 g (4 oz)
  Cheddar cheese,
  grated

Shred the cabbage and cook in a little boiling salted water for 5 minutes; drain.

Chop the onion. Mix all the vegetables together and turn into a well buttered 1.2 litre (2 pint) ovenproof dish.

Cover with the grated cheese and bake in a preheated moderately hot oven, 200°C (400°F), Gas Mark 6, for 20 to 25 minutes, until golden and bubbling. Serve immediately.
Serves 4 to 6

Mixed Stir-fry; Rumbledethumps; Aubergine Fritters

MOCHA BOMBE

250 g (8 oz) plain
   chocolate, chopped
COFFEE ICE CREAM:
2 tablespoons instant
   coffee powder
2 tablespoons boiling
   water
2 egg whites
125 g (4 oz) caster
   sugar
284 ml (10 fl oz)
   double cream

Melt the chocolate in a heatproof bowl over a pan of simmering water.

Put a 1.2 litre (2 pint) basin in the freezer to chill for 10 minutes. Pour the chocolate into the basin and rotate to coat the inside completely. Place the basin in a bowl of crushed ice and continue rotating until the chocolate has set in a layer.

To make the ice cream, mix the coffee with the water; leave to cool. Whisk the egg whites until stiff, then gradually whisk in the sugar. Whip the cream with the coffee mixture until it forms soft peaks. Fold into the meringue mixture.

Spoon into the chocolate mould, smooth the top evenly, cover with foil and freeze until firm.

Dip the basin into cold water, invert onto a serving plate and give a sharp shake to turn out.

Serves 6 to 8

TRUFFLE COFFEE RIPPLE

TRUFFLE MIXTURE:
125 g (4 oz) plain
   chocolate, chopped
2 tablespoons single
   cream
2 tablespoons rum
COFFEE ICE CREAM:
2 tablespoons instant
   coffee powder
2 tablespoons boiling
   water
2 egg whites
125 g (4 oz) caster
   sugar
284 ml (10 fl oz)
   double cream

Put the truffle ingredients in a heatproof bowl over a pan of simmering water until the chocolate has melted. Mix well, then leave to cool.

Meanwhile, make the ice cream: dissolve the coffee in the water and leave to cool. Whisk the egg whites until stiff, then gradually whisk in the sugar. Whip the cream with the coffee until it forms soft peaks. Fold into the meringue mixture.

When the truffle mixture begins to thicken, stir until smooth and soft. Fold into the ice cream mixture, very lightly to create a marbled effect. Turn into a rigid freezerproof container, cover, seal and freeze until firm.

Transfer to the refrigerator 15 minutes before serving, to soften. Scoop into chilled glasses to serve. Alternatively, serve with a chocolate sauce, if preferred.

Serves 8

ICED CHOCOLATE SOUFFLÉS

4 eggs, separated
125 g (4 oz) icing
    sugar, sifted
75 g (3 oz) plain
    chocolate, chopped
1 tablespoon water
250 ml (8 fl oz)
    double cream
2 tablespoons rum
grated chocolate to
    decorate

Tie a double band of foil very tightly around 6 freezerproof ramekin dishes to stand 2.5 cm (1 inch) above the rim.

Place the egg yolks and icing sugar in a bowl and whisk with an electric mixer until thick and creamy.

Place the chocolate and water in a small pan and heat very gently until melted. Cool slightly, then whisk into the egg mixture.

Whip the cream with the rum until it stands in soft peaks, then fold in the chocolate mixture.

Whisk the egg whites until stiff and carefully fold into the mousse. Pour into the prepared ramekins and freeze for 4 hours until firm.

Transfer to the refrigerator 10 minutes before serving to soften. Remove the foil carefully. Sprinkle the chocolate over the top to cover completely.
Serves 4 to 6

CHOCOLATE MINT ICE

2 egg whites
125 g (4 oz) caster
    sugar
1 × 410 g (14.5 oz)
    can evaporated
    milk, chilled
4 drops of green food
    colouring
½ teaspoon
    peppermint essence
75 g (3 oz) plain
    chocolate, finely
    chopped

Whisk the egg whites until stiff, then gradually whisk in the sugar. Place the evaporated milk in a bowl with the colouring and peppermint essence. Whisk until thick, then fold into the meringue mixture with the chocolate.

Turn into a rigid freezerproof container, cover, seal and freeze for 2 hours.

Remove from the freezer and stir vigorously. Re-freeze until firm.

Transfer to the refrigerator 1 hour before serving to soften. Scoop into chilled glass dishes and serve with dessert biscuits or wafers.
Serves 8

OPPOSITE: *Mocha Bombe; Truffle Coffee Ripple*
RIGHT: *Iced Chocolate Soufflés; Chocolate Mint Ice*

STRAWBERRY ICE CREAM

4 egg yolks
1/2 × 340 g (12 oz)
  jar strawberry
  conserve
284 ml (10 fl oz)
  double cream
2 tablespoons brandy
  (optional)

Whisk the egg yolks in a warmed bowl for at least 5 minutes, until pale and thick. Add the conserve and whisk again.

Beat the cream, with the brandy if using, until it forms soft peaks. Fold into the strawberry mixture and turn into a rigid freezerproof container. Cover and freeze until firm.

Scoop into chilled individual dishes to serve.
Serves 6

CRÈME BRÛLÉE

284 ml (10 fl oz)
  double cream
12 drops vanilla
  essence
2 egg yolks
125 g (4 oz) caster
  sugar

Place the cream and vanilla essence in a small pan and heat very gently. Whisk the egg yolks with 2 teaspoons of the sugar in a heatproof basin. Stir in the cream and stand the basin over a pan of simmering water. Stir constantly until the mixture thickens slightly.

Pour into 4 ramekin dishes and bake in a preheated moderate oven, 160°C (325°F), Gas Mark 3, for 8 minutes. Cool slightly, then place in the refrigerator until thoroughly chilled, preferably overnight.

Sprinkle evenly with the remaining sugar and place under a preheated hot grill until the sugar has caramelized. Cool, then chill for about 2 hours before serving.
Serves 4

ORANGE SORBET

175 g (6 oz) caster
  sugar
450 ml (3/4 pint)
  water
6 large oranges
1 tablespoon lemon
  juice
3 egg whites,
  whisked
shredded orange rind
  to decorate

Place the sugar and water in a pan and heat gently, stirring until dissolved. Bring to the boil, simmer for 15 minutes, then leave to cool.

Cut off the tops of the oranges. Using a sharp knife, remove as much flesh from the insides as possible. Reserve the orange shells.

Add the flesh to the syrup with the lemon juice, then sieve into a rigid freezerproof container. Cover, seal and freeze for about 2 hours, until mushy.

Whisk the egg whites into the orange mixture. Spoon into the orange shells and place in a freezer-proof container; freeze until firm.

Transfer to the refrigerator 1 hour before serving to soften. Decorate with shredded orange rind to serve.
Serves 6

LEFT: *Crème Brûlée; Orange Sorbet; Strawberry Ice Cream*
OPPOSITE: *Iced Zabaione; Mango Ice Cream; Gooseberry Ice Cream*

ICED ZABAIONE

4 egg yolks
75 g (3 oz) icing
  sugar, sifted
4 tablespoons
  Marsala
120 ml (4 fl oz)
  double cream
chopped pistachio
  nuts to decorate

Place the egg yolks in a bowl with the icing sugar and whisk with an electric mixer until thick and mousse-like. Whip the Marsala and cream together until thick, then carefully fold into the egg mixture.

Pour into 4 freezerproof ramekin dishes, cover, seal and freeze. Sprinkle with chopped nuts to serve.

Serves 4

MANGO ICE CREAM

2 ripe mangoes
284 ml (10 fl oz)
  single cream
125 g (4 oz) icing
  sugar, sifted
juice of 2 limes or
  small lemons

Cut the mangoes in half lengthways, scrape out the flesh and discard the stones. Place the flesh in an electric blender or food processor with the remaining ingredients and work to a purée. Pour into a rigid freezerproof container, cover, seal and freeze for 2 hours. Remove from the freezer, whisk well, then re-freeze until firm.

Transfer to the refrigerator 30 minutes before serving to soften. Scoop into chilled glasses to serve.

Serves 6 to 8

GOOSEBERRY ICE CREAM

500 g (1 lb)
  gooseberries
125 g (4 oz) caster
  sugar
2 tablespoons water
3 egg whites
75 g (3 oz) icing
  sugar, sifted
few drops of green
  food colouring
142 ml (5 fl oz)
  double cream,
  whipped
frosted mint leaves to
  decorate

Place the gooseberries in a pan with the sugar and water. Cover and cook gently for 10 to 15 minutes until tender. Purée in a blender or food processor, then sieve. Leave to cool.

Whisk the egg whites until stiff, then gradually whisk in the icing sugar. Fold in the purée, food colouring and cream.

Turn into a rigid freezerproof container, cover, seal and freeze.

Transfer to the refrigerator 30 minutes before serving to soften. Scoop into chilled glasses and decorate with frosted mint leaves.

Serves 6 to 8

AVOCADO ICE CREAM

2 ripe avocados,
   peeled and stoned
142 ml (5 fl oz)
   single cream
284 ml (10 fl oz)
   double cream
75 g (3 oz) caster
   sugar
juice of ½ lemon
50 g (2 oz) split
   almonds, finely
   chopped and
   toasted

Place the avocados and single cream in an electric blender and work until smooth.

Whip the double cream until it forms soft peaks. Fold in the sugar, avocado mixture, lemon juice and almonds. Place in a rigid freezerproof container. Cover, seal and freeze.

Transfer to the refrigerator 30 minutes before serving to soften. Scoop into 4 chilled glasses.
Serves 4

BOMBE GRAND MARNIER

426 ml (15 fl oz)
   double cream
142 ml (5 fl oz)
   single cream
100 g (4 oz)
   meringues
2 tablespoons Grand
   Marnier
1 tablespoon icing
   sugar, sifted
TO DECORATE:
142 ml (5 fl oz)
   double cream
finely shredded
   orange rind,
   blanched and dried

Whip the double and single creams together until the mixture forms soft peaks. Break the meringues into pieces and fold into the cream, together with the Grand Marnier and icing sugar. Turn into a 1.2 litre (2 pint) freezerproof pudding basin, cover with foil and freeze until firm.

Turn out onto a serving dish 45 minutes before serving. Decorate with piped cream rosettes and orange rind shreds. Leave in the refrigerator until required.
Serves 8

RASPBERRY PARFAIT

500 g (1 lb)
   raspberries
2 egg whites
125 g (4 oz) caster
   sugar
284 ml (10 fl oz)
   double cream,
   lightly whipped
1 tablespoon
   Cointreau
crisp biscuits to serve

Rub the raspberries through a sieve or work in an electric blender until smooth and sieve to remove pips. Place in a rigid freezerproof container. Cover, seal and freeze for 1 to 2 hours, until half-frozen.

Whisk the egg whites until stiff. Whisk in the sugar, a tablespoon at a time; the mixture should be very stiff.

Beat the half-frozen purée with a fork. Fold the cream into the egg white mixture, then carefully fold in the half-frozen purée and the Cointreau.

Spoon into chilled glasses and serve immediately with crisp biscuits.
Serves 4 to 6

Raspberry Parfait; Avocado Ice Cream; Bombe Grand Marnier

CHAMPAGNE SORBET

300 g (10 oz) sugar
250 ml (8 fl oz) water
600 ml (1 pint) sparkling white wine
3 tablespoons lemon juice
2 egg whites
4 tablespoons icing sugar

Dissolve the sugar in the water in a saucepan over low heat, then bring to the boil. Boil for about 5 minutes or until thick but not beginning to brown. Cool, then stir in 350 ml (12 fl oz) of the wine and the lemon juice. Pour into freezer trays and freeze for about 1 hour or until mushy.

Pour the mixture into a bowl and beat well for 2 minutes. Return to the freezer trays and freeze for a further 30 minutes. Beat again. Repeat the freezing and beating every 30 minutes for the next 2 hours.

Beat the egg whites until stiff. Gradually beat in the icing sugar.

Beat the frozen mixture well to break down the ice crystals, then fold in the meringue. Return to the freezer and freeze until firm.

About 30 minutes before required, put the sorbet in the refrigerator to soften slightly. Before serving, pour a little of the wine over each portion.
Serves 8

Champagne Sorbet

BISQUIT TORTONI

1 large egg white
284 ml (10 fl oz) double cream
4 tablespoons icing sugar, sifted
3 tablespoons brandy
40 g (1½ oz) flaked almonds, toasted

Whisk egg white until stiff but not dry. Whip cream until beginning to thicken, add half the icing sugar and half the brandy; whip until thick. Repeat with remaining sugar and brandy. Fold in the egg white.

Spoon into 6 or 8 freezerproof sundae dishes and top with the nuts. Place in deep freezerproof containers and cover with a lid or loosely with foil; do not flatten. Freeze for about 3 hours or until firm.

Transfer to the refrigerator about 30 minutes before serving to soften.
Serves 6 to 8

CHOCOLATE BOMBE NOËL

125 g (4 oz) glacé cherries, chopped
125 g (4 oz) raisins
50 g (2 oz) angelica, chopped
50 g (2 oz) crystalized pineapple (optional)
50 g (2 oz) sultanas
6 tablespoons rum
3 egg yolks
75 g (3 oz) caster sugar
175 g (6 oz) plain chocolate, chopped
284 ml (10 fl oz) single cream
284 ml (10 fl oz) double cream, whipped
125 g (4 oz) blanched almonds, chopped and toasted

Place the fruit in a bowl, stir in the rum and leave to soak for 1 hour.

Beat the egg yolks and sugar in a heatproof bowl, using an electric whisk, until thick and mousse-like. Gently melt the chocolate in a pan with the single cream, then beat to just below boiling point. Beat into the egg yolk mixture. Place over a pan of simmering water and stir until thickened. Strain and cool.

Fold the custard into half the double cream. Pour into a rigid freezerproof container, cover, seal and freeze for 2 hours. Remove from the freezer.

Stir well and mix in the fruit, rum and almonds. Turn into a 1.75 litre (3 pint) pudding basin, cover with foil, seal and freeze until firm.

Dip the basin into cold water and turn out onto a chilled plate. Smooth the surface and decorate with the remaining cream and a sprig of holly.
Serves 6 to 8

PETITS VACHERINS AUX NOIX

MERINGUE:
2 egg whites
125 g (4 oz) soft brown sugar
50 g (2 oz) walnuts, ground

FILLING:
2 tablespoons rum
142 ml (5 fl oz) double cream

TO DECORATE:
6 walnut halves

Whisk the egg whites until stiff, then whisk in the sugar, a tablespoon at a time. Carefully fold in the walnuts.

Line two baking sheets with silicone paper and draw six 7.5 cm (3 inch) circles and six 5 cm (2 inch) circles. Put the meringue into a piping bag fitted with a 1 cm (½ inch) plain nozzle and pipe onto the circles to cover completely.

Bake in a preheated very cool oven, 120°C (250°F), Gas Mark ½, for 1½ to 2 hours. Transfer to a wire rack to cool.

Place the rum and cream in a bowl and whip until stiff. Put into a piping bag fitted with a large fluted nozzle and pipe three-quarters onto the larger circles. Cover with the small circles. Decorate with the remaining cream and the walnut halves.

Serves 6

APPLE AND WALNUT WHIRLS

75 g (3 oz) butter
50 g (2 oz) soft brown sugar
125 g (4 oz) plain flour, sifted
75 g (3 oz) walnuts, ground

FILLING:
1 tablespoon apricot jam
500 g (1 lb) dessert apples, peeled, cored and sliced
½ teaspoon ground cinnamon
250 ml (8 fl oz) double cream, whipped

TO DECORATE:
chopped walnuts

Cream the butter and sugar together until light and fluffy. Stir in the flour and walnuts, and mix to a firm dough, using your hand. Turn onto a floured surface and knead lightly until smooth. Roll the dough out thinly; cut out ten 7.5 cm (3 inch) and ten 5 cm (2 inch) circles. Place on a baking sheet and bake in a preheated moderate oven, 180°C (350°F), Gas Mark 4, for 12 to 15 minutes, until golden. Transfer to a wire rack to cool.

Place the jam and apples in a pan, cover and cook gently for 15 to 20 minutes, until softened. Add the cinnamon and leave to cool.

Spread the cooled apple mixture over the larger rounds, pipe two thirds of the cream over the apple and top with the small circles. Decorate with remaining cream and walnuts.

Serves 10

ZUCOTTO

1 quantity chocolate
  whisked sponge
  mixture (see page
  150)
4 tablespoons brandy
426 ml (15 fl oz)
  double cream
40 g (1½ oz) icing
  sugar, sifted
50 g (2 oz) plain
  chocolate, chopped
25 g (1 oz) almonds,
  chopped and
  toasted
175 g (6 oz) black
  cherries, stoned
2 tablespoons kirsch
1 tablespoon cocoa
  powder, sifted

Spoon the sponge mixture into a lined and greased 20 cm (8 inch) cake tin. Bake in a preheated moderate oven, 180°C (350°F), Gas Mark 4, for 35 to 40 minutes. Turn onto a wire rack to cool.

Split the sponge in half and line a 1.2 litre (2 pint) pudding basin with one layer, shaping it to fit. Sprinkle the sides with the brandy; set aside.

Whip the cream until it forms soft peaks. Fold in 25 g (1 oz) of the icing sugar, the chocolate, almonds, cherries and kirsch. Spoon into the basin and top with the remaining sponge. Cover with a plate and chill for 2 to 3 hours.

Run a palette knife around the sides of the bowl and turn out onto a plate. Sprinkle with the remaining icing sugar and cocoa powder to make a pattern.
Serves 6 to 8

MALAKOFF GÂTEAU

75 g (3 oz) butter
75 g (3 oz) caster
  sugar
1 egg yolk
125 g (4 oz) ground
  almonds
90 ml (3 fl oz) single
  cream
3 tablespoons brandy
300 ml (½ pint) cold
  strong black coffee
24 sponge fingers
142 ml (5 fl oz)
  double cream,
  whipped
toasted flaked
  almonds to decorate

Cream the butter and sugar together until light and fluffy. Add the egg yolk, almonds and single cream and beat until smooth.

Add the brandy to the coffee and quickly dip in the sponge fingers. Arrange some in the base of a lined and greased 500 g (1 lb) loaf tin.

Spread half the almond mixture on top. Repeat these layers once more, then finish with a layer of sponge fingers. Chill in the refrigerator until set.

Spread two-thirds of the cream over the gâteau. Pipe cream on top and sprinkle with almonds to decorate.
Serves 6 to 8

OPPOSITE: *Petits Vacherins aux Noix; Apple and Walnut Whirls*
RIGHT: *Hazelnut Shortcake*

HAZELNUT SHORTCAKE

HAZELNUT PASTRY:
75 g (3 oz)
  margarine or butter
50 g (2 oz)
  muscovado sugar
100 g (4 oz)
  wholemeal flour
75 g (3 oz) hazelnuts,
  ground and roasted
egg white for
  brushing
1 tablespoon chopped
  hazelnuts
FILLING:
500 g (1 lb) dessert
  apples, peeled,
  cored and sliced
2 tablespoons apple
  juice
50 g (2 oz) raisins
50 g (2 oz) sultanas
1 teaspoon ground
  mixed spice

Beat the fat and sugar together until soft. Stir in the flour and ground hazelnuts and mix to a firm dough. Turn onto a floured surface and knead lightly until smooth. Divide in half and roll each piece into a 20 cm (8 inch) round on a baking sheet. Brush one round with egg white and sprinkle with the chopped nuts.

Bake both rounds in a preheated moderately hot oven, 190°C (375°F), Gas Mark 5, for 10 to 15 minutes. Cut the nut-covered round into 8 sections while still warm. Transfer both rounds to a wire rack to cool.

Place the apples and juice in a pan, cover and cook gently for 15 minutes, stirring occasionally. Add the remaining ingredients and leave to cool.

Spread over the hazelnut round and arrange the cut triangles on top. Serve with whipped cream
Serves 6 to 8

PRALINE CHARLOTTE

PRALINE:
50 g (2 oz) whole
  almonds
50 g (2 oz) caster
  sugar
CHARLOTTE:
18 sponge fingers
3 egg yolks
3 tablespoons icing
  sugar, sifted
350 ml (12 fl oz)
  milk
15 g (½ oz)
  gelatine, soaked in
  3 tablespoons cold
  water
284 ml (10 fl oz)
  whipping cream,
  whipped
TO FINISH:
4 tablespoons double
  cream, whipped

First make the praline. Heat the almonds and sugar in a pan gently until melted, then cook until nut brown. Turn onto an oiled baking sheet. When hard, crush with a rolling pin.

Trim one end off each sponge finger to the height of a 1.5 litre (2½ pint) charlotte mould. Fit them closely, rounded end down, around the side of the lightly oiled mould.

Beat the egg yolks and icing sugar together until creamy. Bring the milk to the boil, then stir into the egg mixture. Return to the pan and cook gently, stirring until thickened. Strain into a bowl, add the gelatine and stir until dissolved. Cool.

Add three quarters of the praline and stir over a bowl of iced water until the mixture starts to thicken. Fold in the cream, pour into the prepared mould and chill until set.

To serve, invert onto a plate and decorate with the cream and remaining praline.
Serves 6

CHARLOTTE RUSSE

600 ml (1 pint) made
  lemon jelly, cool
  but liquid
½ glacé cherry
few angelica
  diamonds
16 sponge fingers
CREAM FILLING:
3 egg yolks
25 g (1 oz) caster
  sugar
300 ml (½ pint)
  milk
15 g (½ oz) gelatine,
  soaked in 3
  tablespoons cold
  water
3 drops of vanilla
  essence
250 ml (8 fl oz)
  double cream,
  whipped

Pour a little jelly into a 1.2 litre (2 pint) charlotte mould to a depth of 5 mm (¼ inch) and chill until set. Arrange the cherry and angelica on the jelly and set in position with a little more jelly. Allow the remaining jelly to set, then chop finely.

Trim one rounded end off the sponge fingers and arrange to fit closely around the side of the mould.

To make the filling: Beat the egg yolks and sugar together until creamy. Bring the milk to the boil, then stir into the egg mixture. Stir over a low heat until thickened.

Strain the custard into a bowl, add the soaked gelatine and the essence and stir until dissolved. Cool, then stir over a bowl of iced water until the mixture starts to thicken. Fold in the cream. Pour into the mould, cover and chill in the refrigerator overnight.

To serve, invert onto a plate and arrange the jelly around the base.
Serves 6

USING CREAM FOR DECORATION

Many dessert recipes are topped with cream – to ensure a really professional finish follow the tips below:
- When whipping double or whipping cream make sure that the cream, bowl and whisk are all cold.
- Use a balloon or rotary whisk and whip quickly at first until the cream begins to thicken, then slowly until thick enough to stand in soft peaks. Do not overwhip or the cream will start to separate and lose its shine.
- Extend cream by adding single cream to double if liked – but never add more than half the quantity of single to double.
- When whipping cream for piping only whip until just stiff – the cream thickens further when being piped, from the warmth of the hands on the piping bag.
- To fill a piping bag, rest the bag in a large jar with the bag folded over the rim of the jar. Hold the bag above the cream and squeeze gently downwards to pipe rosettes, stars and shells for example.

LEFT: *Praline Charlotte*
OPPOSITE: *Praline Peach Gâteau; Pineapple Pavlova*

PRALINE PEACH GÂTEAU

3 eggs
75 g (3 oz) caster
    sugar
grated rind of 1 lemon
75 g (3 oz) plain
    flour, sifted
PRALINE:
50 g (2 oz) whole
    almonds
50 g (2 oz) caster
    sugar
TO FINISH:
284 ml (10 fl oz)
    double cream,
    whipped
4 tablespoons apricot
    jam
2 teaspoons water
2 peaches, stoned and
    sliced

Place the eggs, sugar and lemon rind in a bowl and whisk with an electric mixer until thick and mousse-like. Carefully fold in the flour, then turn into a lined, greased and floured deep 20 cm (8 inch) cake tin.

Bake in a preheated moderately hot oven, 190°C (375°F), Gas Mark 5, for 30 to 35 minutes, until the cake springs back when lightly pressed. Turn onto a wire rack to cool.

Make the praline as for Praline Charlotte (see opposite) and fold half into two thirds of the cream. Split the cake in half and sandwich together with the praline cream.

Heat the jam with the water, sieve, reheat and use three quarters to glaze the side of the cake. Press the remaining praline around the side.

Arrange the peaches, overlapping, in a circle on top, leaving a border around the edge. Reheat remaining glaze and brush over the peaches.

Pipe the remaining cream in a decorative border around the edge.
Serves 6

PINEAPPLE PAVLOVA

4 egg whites
250 g (8 oz) caster
    sugar
1 tablespoon
    cornflour
2 teaspoons vinegar
125 g (4 oz)
    hazelnuts, ground
    and toasted
FILLING:
1 small pineapple,
    thinly sliced
3 tablespoons kirsch
284 ml (10 fl oz)
    double cream
3 kiwi fruit, sliced

Whisk the egg whites until stiff. Add the sugar a tablespoon at a time, whisking until the meringue is very stiff. Whisk in the cornflour and vinegar, then carefully fold in the hazelnuts.

Pile the meringue onto a baking sheet lined with silicone paper and spread into a 20 cm (8 inch) round; hollow out the centre slightly. Bake in a preheated cool oven, 150°C (300°F), Gas Mark 2, for 1 hour. Leave to cool, peel off the paper and place on a serving dish.

Meanwhile, place the pineapple slices in a shallow dish, sprinkle with the kirsch and leave for 1 hour.

Place the cream in a bowl and add the kirsch from the pineapple. Whip until stiff, then spoon onto the pavlova, spreading to the edges.

Arrange some kiwi fruit slices overlapping in a circle around the edge. Lay the pineapple slices overlapping inside and finish with kiwi fruit in the centre.
Serves 8

KISSEL CUP

250 g (8 oz) mixed
  blackcurrants and
  redcurrants
50 g (2 oz) caster
  sugar
4 tablespoons water
grated rind and juice
  of ½ orange
125 g (4 oz)
  raspberries
125 g (4 oz)
  strawberries, sliced
1 teaspoon arrowroot
4 tablespoons brandy
250 ml (8 fl oz)
  whipping cream
1 tablespoon icing
  sugar, sifted
redcurrants to
  decorate

Place the currants in a pan with the caster sugar, water and orange rind. Bring to the boil and simmer gently for 10 minutes, until softened.

Strain, reserving the syrup. Place the currants in a bowl with the raspberries and strawberries.

Return the syrup to the pan and bring to the boil. Mix the arrowroot with the orange juice and stir into the boiling syrup. Cook, stirring, until thickened and clear. Pour over the fruit with 2 tablespoons of the brandy, mix well and leave to cool.

Spoon the fruit mixture into glasses. Whip the cream with the remaining brandy and the icing sugar and spoon over the fruit mixture. Chill and decorate with redcurrants to serve.
Serves 6

PINEAPPLE ROMANOFF

1 large pineapple
50 g (2 oz) icing
  sugar, sifted
grated rind of ½
  orange
3 tablespoons
  Curaçao or
  Cointreau
250 g (8 oz)
  strawberries
284 ml (10 fl oz)
  double cream

Cut the pineapple in half lengthways, scoop out the flesh, discarding the central core, and cut into cubes. Reserve the shells. Place the cubes in a bowl with the icing sugar and orange rind. Pour over the Curaçao or Cointreau and leave to soak for 2 hours.

Set aside a few strawberries for decoration; slice the remainder. Whip the cream until it holds its shape, then fold in the sliced strawberries and the pineapple mixture.

Spoon into the pineapple shells, decorate with the reserved strawberries and chill for 30 minutes before serving.
Serves 4 to 6

ALMOND CRÈME BRÛLÉE

4 egg yolks
1 tablespoon caster
  sugar
568 ml (1 pint)
  double cream
few drops of vanilla
  essence
TO FINISH:
4 tablespoons
  chopped almonds
3 tablespoons soft
  brown sugar

Beat the egg yolks and sugar together. Warm the cream in a double saucepan or heatproof bowl over a pan of simmering water. Pour onto the egg mixture and stir well. Return to the pan or bowl and heat gently, stirring constantly, until thick enough to coat the back of a spoon. Add the vanilla essence.

Strain into 6 ramekin dishes and place in a roasting pan containing 2.5 cm (1 inch) water. Cook in a preheated cool oven, 140°C (275°F), Gas Mark 1, for 30 to 40 minutes.

Remove the ramekins, cool, then chill in the refrigerator overnight. Mix the almonds with the sugar and sprinkle over the custards to cover completely. Place under a preheated hot grill until the sugar caramelizes. Cool, then chill in the refrigerator for 1 hour before serving.
Serves 6

ZABAIONE WITH MACAROONS

4 macaroons
4 egg yolks
75 g (3 oz) caster
  sugar
4 tablespoons
  Marsala

Break the macaroons into small pieces and divide equally between 4 glasses.

Place the egg yolks in a bowl with the sugar and Marsala. Whisk together on high speed over a pan of gently simmering water until thick and mousse-like.

Pour over the macaroons and serve immediately, while the zabaione is still warm.
Serves 4

Pineapple Romanoff

Summer Pudding

SUMMER PUDDING

500 g (1 lb) mixed
    soft fruit
    (raspberries,
    redcurrants,
    blackberries,
    strawberries,
    blackcurrants, etc.)
125 g (4 oz) caster
    sugar
6 thin slices white
    bread, crusts
    removed

Put the fruit in a saucepan with the sugar and simmer gently, stirring occasionally, for about 10 minutes, until tender but not mushy.

Cut one circle of bread to fit the base of a 900 ml (1½ pint) pudding basin, one for the middle and one to fit the top. Cut the remaining bread in half lengthwise. Place the small circle in the basin. Line the sides with the slices of bread. Pour in half of the fruit and cover with the middle circle. Top with remaining fruit, then the large circle of bread.

Put the basin on a plate, cover with a saucer and put a weight on top. Leave in a cool place overnight.

Turn out onto a serving plate and serve with cream.

Serves 6

SHRIKAND

1 kg (2.2 lb) natural
    yogurt
1 packet powdered
    saffron
about 2 tablespoons
    caster sugar
about 1 tablespoon
    rose water
TO DECORATE:
1 teaspoon cardamom
    seeds, crushed
1 tablespoon pistachio
    nuts, shelled and
    chopped

Turn the yogurt into a strainer lined with muslin and leave to drip over a bowl for 6 hours. Put the dried curds – there will be about 300 g (10 oz) – into a bowl and beat in the saffron. Add sugar to taste. Mix in the rose water, a little at a time, until the mixture resembles thick cream. Cover and chill until required.

Spoon into individual bowls and decorate with the cardamom and pistachio nuts. Serve as a delicious dessert to round off an Indian meal.
Serves 4

ORANGE SYLLABUB

grated rind and juice
    of 2 oranges
grated rind and juice
    of 1 lemon
75 g (3 oz) caster
    sugar
2 tablespoons
    Cointreau
284 ml (10 fl oz)
    double cream

Place the orange and lemon rinds in a bowl with the juices and sugar. Add the Cointreau and leave for 1 hour.

Add the orange mixture to the cream and whisk on medium speed until it holds its shape. Pour into glasses and chill until required. Serve with crisp biscuits.
Serves 6

FREEZING DESSERTS

A few well chosen desserts, packed away in the freezer, can make or save the day if unexpected guests arrive or when you are called upon to create a meal at a moment's notice.

Frozen ice creams, mousses, sorbets and fools are a must and can be lifted to the heights of luxury if topped with fruity sauces, swirls of cream or fresh fruits.

Freeze too those seasonal favourites that rely upon windfalls or gluts of fruit – desserts like Summer Pudding (left) – heavily laden with raspberries, redcurrants, blackberries, strawberries or blackcurrants; or Apple and Walnut Whirls (page 60) – biscuit rounds and filling frozen separately then easily assembled when required; or Almond Fruit Salad (page 67) – made when apples, peaches, strawberries and pineapple are plentiful.

Freeze in rigid boxes or wrapped in foil. Seal well and label carefully. Packed this way most desserts will keep for up to 6 months.

HAZELNUT AND WHISKY WHIP

50 g (2 oz)
    hazelnuts, skinned
    and finely chopped
50 g (2 oz) demerara
    sugar
50 g (2 oz)
    wholemeal
    breadcrumbs
284 ml (10 fl oz)
    double cream
150 g (5.2 oz)
    natural yogurt
3 tablespoons whisky
1 tablespoon clear
    honey

Combine the hazelnuts, sugar and breadcrumbs and place on a baking sheet. Put under a preheated hot grill until golden brown, stirring frequently. Leave to cool.

Whip the cream until it stands in soft peaks then whip in the yogurt, whisky and honey.

Fold in the hazelnut mixture, spoon into individual dishes and chill before serving.
Serves 6 to 8

PEACH AND PASSION FRUIT CHANTILLY

3 passion fruit
6 peaches, skinned,
    halved and stoned
120 ml (4 fl oz)
    double cream
2 tablespoons orange
    flower water
    (optional)

Cut the passion fruit in half using a sharp knife, and scoop out the flesh into a bowl. Slice the peaches thinly and add to the bowl. Carefully toss the fruit together until combined and spoon into 4 individual glasses or serving dishes.

Whip the cream together with the orange flower water, if using, until it stands in soft peaks. Spoon a little cream onto each fruit salad before serving.
Serves 4
NOTE: Passion fruit are ready to eat when their skins are dimpled. The whole flesh, including the pips, may be eaten.

ALMOND FRUIT SALAD

4 dessert apples, cored
4 peaches, skinned
    and stoned
125 g (4 oz)
    strawberries
4 slices pineapple
125 g (4 oz) lychees,
    skinned
ALMOND SYRUP:
2 tablespoons ground
    almonds
450 ml (¾ pint)
    water
1 tablespoon cornflour,
    blended with 2
    tablespoons water
3 tablespoons sugar

First, make the syrup. Put the almonds, water, blended cornflour and sugar in a pan and mix well. Gradually bring to the boil, stirring, then simmer for 10 minutes, stirring constantly. Remove from the heat and leave to cool, stirring occasionally to prevent a skin forming.

Slice the apples, peaches and strawberries; cut the pineapple into cubes. Put all the fruit in a bowl and mix well. Spoon over the almond syrup and chill before serving.
Serves 4 to 6

Peach and Passion Fruit Chantilly

BARBECUE PARTIES

Perhaps it is the al fresco nature of eating food out-of-doors, or the sight and aroma of food sizzling on a grill that makes barbecues such irresistible fun. Certainly, if the weather is good, and numbers are not too large, there are few parties easier to plan and enjoy.

The basics of barbecuing are really quite simple. You will need cooking and serving equipment, fuel and food and a place to eat. You may have a purpose-built barbecue like a simple hibachi, sophisticated gas or electric wagon model or own-built brick, or improvise with an old metal wheelbarrow and grid or beach pebbles and chicken wire – whatever the type it must be located in an attractive but practical place. Wherever you choose, make sure it is well-lit, well-drained and shaded from any strong breezes. Keep well away from trees, shrubs and wooden buildings.

Charcoal is the most popular fuel, either lumpwood or briquette, but wood can be used. As basics, arm yourself with a set of tongs, oven gloves and a sprinkler – to douse over-exuberant flames. Cooking foil, basting brushes, spatulas and aprons will be useful.

Although a barbecue is designed to be an impromptu affair, it is wise to prepare some of the food beforehand. Marinate meat, fish and poultry, and prepare salads, sauces and relishes well ahead. Also put to chill or on ice a few simple desserts. A word of warning – fresh air certainly sharpens appetites so it is the wise hostess who thinks of average indoor appetites and then doubles them!

Finally, expect the unexpected – a summer downpour. Make plans to move indoors if necessary, and have at hand a makeshift canvas covering or umbrella to protect the barbecue if it rains.

BEAN SOUP

125 g (4 oz) haricot
  beans
50 g (2 oz) each red
  kidney beans and
  dried peas
2 large onions
2 celery sticks
2 large carrots
25 g (1 oz) butter
2 cloves garlic, crushed
1 × 397 g (14 oz)
  can tomatoes
120 ml (4 fl oz) dry
  red wine
300 ml (½ pint) stock
1 bouquet garni
salt and pepper
125 g (4 oz)
  courgettes, sliced
1 tablespoon Worcester-
  shire sauce
1 tablespoon tomato
  purée
PISTOU:
4 cloves garlic
1 bunch basil
4 tablespoons olive oil
25 g (1 oz) pine nuts

Soak all the pulses separately in cold water overnight. Rinse in cold water and drain. Put in a large pan, cover with cold water and bring to the boil; do not add salt at this stage. Boil steadily for 10 minutes, then cover and simmer for 1¼ hours or until the beans are tender; drain.

Chop the onions, celery and carrots. Melt the butter in a large pan, add the onions and fry until golden. Add the garlic, celery and carrots, tomatoes with their juice, the wine, stock, bouquet garni and salt and pepper to taste. Bring to the boil, cover and simmer for 20 minutes, then stir in the courgettes, Worcestershire sauce and tomato purée. Continue cooking for 5 minutes, then add the cooked beans and peas; heat through.

Meanwhile, make the pistou. Pound the garlic with the basil, oil and nuts to a smooth paste. Mix into the soup just before serving.

Serve with grated Cheddar cheese and crusty rolls.
Serves 6 to 8

COURGETTE SOUP

25 g (1 oz) butter
2 large onions,
  chopped
750 g (1½ lb)
  courgettes, chopped
2 × 411 g (14½ oz)
  cans consommé
2 tablespoons dry
  sherry
1 bouquet garni
salt and pepper
142 ml (5 fl oz)
  double cream
croûtons to garnish

Melt the butter in a pan, add the onions and cook gently for 5 minutes. Stir in the courgettes and cook gently for 10 minutes.

Stir in the consommé and sherry and bring to the boil. Add the bouquet garni and seasoning, cover and simmer for 30 minutes.

Remove the bouquet garni and cool slightly. Sieve or work in an electric blender or food processor until smooth. Return to the pan and heat through.

Stir in the cream and serve, garnished with croûtons.
Serves 6

PRAWN CHOWDER

125 g (4 oz) streaky
   bacon, derinded
   and chopped
4 potatoes, chopped
1 large onion, finely
   chopped
25 g (1 oz) plain
   flour
½ teaspoon curry
   powder
600 ml (1 pint) water
salt and pepper
250 g (8 oz) peeled
   prawns, fresh,
   canned and
   drained, or frozen
   and thawed
600 ml (1 pint) milk
4 tablespoons dry
   sherry (optional)
2 tablespoons
   chopped parsley to
   garnish

Place the bacon in a large pan and heat gently until the fat runs. Increase the heat and when the bacon begins to brown, add the potatoes and onion. Fry for 5 minutes, then stir in the flour and curry powder. Gradually add the water, stirring constantly. Season with salt and pepper to taste and bring to the boil, stirring. Add the prawns and simmer for 30 minutes, until the potato is tender.

Pour in the milk and sherry, if using, and heat through gently. Check the seasoning and sprinkle with chopped parsley just before serving.
Serves 8

CHILLED SHERRIED GRAPEFRUIT

Prepare this refreshing starter a few hours before the barbecue, for convenience.

4 grapefruit
125 g (4 oz)
   demerara sugar
4 tablespoons sherry

Halve the grapefruit, loosen the segments with a serrated knife and snip out the core with scissors. Sprinkle 15 g (½ oz) of the sugar and ½ tablespoon of the sherry over each half.

Cover the grapefruit halves with cling film and chill for at least 1 hour before serving.
Serves 8

OPPOSITE: *Bean Soup; Courgette Soup*
RIGHT: *Prawn Chowder; Chilled Sherried Grapefruit*

SPARE RIBS WITH GINGER

1 kg (2 lb) pork
    spare ribs
SAUCE:
2 spring onions,
    chopped
2 cloves garlic, thinly
    sliced
2.5 cm (1 inch) piece
    root ginger,
    shredded
1 tablespoon soy
    sauce
4 tablespoons clear
    honey
3 tablespoons lemon
    juice
2 tablespoons mango
    chutney
½ teaspoon ground
    ginger
1 tablespoon oil
2 tablespoons dry
    sherry

Put the spare ribs in a roasting pan, cover and cook in a preheated moderately hot oven, 200°C (400°F), Gas Mark 6, for 30 minutes, or on the barbecue grid 10 cm (4 inches) above the coals.

Put all the sauce ingredients in a pan over a low heat, gradually bring to the boil and cook for 1 minute.

Pour off the fat and liquid from the roasting pan, if roasting. Spoon the sauce over the ribs, covering them all well.

Return to the oven or barbecue and cook for 15 to 20 minutes, basting frequently.

Serve hot or cold.
Serves 4 to 6

ORANGE SPARE RIBS

1.5 kg (3 lb) pork
    spare ribs
2 tablespoons clear
    honey
1 tablespoon lemon
    juice
1 tablespoon
    Worcestershire
    sauce
1 teaspoon soy sauce
2 oranges
salt and pepper

Cut the spare ribs into serving pieces. Place the honey, lemon juice, Worcestershire sauce and soy sauce in a small pan. Grate the rind from one orange and add to the pan, together with the juice of both oranges. Add salt and pepper to taste and heat gently, stirring occasionally. Leave to cool, then pour over the meat. Leave to marinate overnight.

Drain and reserve the marinade. Place the spare ribs in a roasting pan and cook in a preheated moderate oven, 180°C (350°F), Gas Mark 4, for 1 hour.

Transfer to the barbecue grid, about 10 cm (4 inches) above the coals. Cook for 15 minutes, turning and basting frequently with the reserved marinade, until crisp.
Serves 8

CHICKEN LIVER AND KIDNEY KEBABS

3 × 227 g (8 oz)
    tubs frozen chicken
    livers, thawed
16 lambs' kidneys,
    skinned, halved
    and cored
bay leaves to taste
salt and pepper
3 tablespoons oil

Thread the livers, kidneys and bay leaves alternately onto 8 skewers. Sprinkle with salt and pepper and brush with oil.

Place the kebabs on the barbecue grid, about 10 cm (4 inches) above the coals, and cook for about 10 minutes, turning frequently.
Serves 8

Spare Ribs with Ginger

SPICY BEEFBURGERS

1 kg (2 lb) minced
   beef
salt
2 tablespoons green
   peppercorns
1 tablespoon chopped
   thyme
2 teaspoons Worcester-
   shire sauce
2 teaspoons French
   mustard
TO SERVE:
8 burger buns
8 lettuce leaves
selection of relishes
1 onion, sliced
4 tomatoes, sliced

Put the beef in a bowl and season well with salt. Stir in the peppercorns, thyme, Worcestershire sauce and mustard; mix well. Divide into 8 portions and form into flat cakes.

Cook under a preheated moderate grill, or on the barbecue grid 10 cm (4 inches) above the coals, for 3 to 5 minutes each side, according to taste.

Cut the buns in half and toast the cut side. Arrange a lettuce leaf on each bun base, top with a burger and relish. Arrange onion and tomato slices on top and replace the bun lid. Serve immediately, in a napkin.
Serves 4 to 8

WINCHESTER SAUSAGES

Sausages are the perfect brunch or barbecue food and these are well worth making.

250 g (8 oz) belly
   pork, minced
250 g (8 oz) lean
   minced pork
25 g (1 oz) pork fat,
   minced
6 tablespoons milk
75 g (3 oz) whole-
   meal breadcrumbs
1 clove garlic, crushed
¼ teaspoon each
   ground mace and
   allspice
1 tablespoon each
   chopped parsley
   and sage
1 teaspoon chopped
   thyme
salt and pepper
about 1 metre (3 ft)
   sausage casing (see
   note)

Mix the pork and fat together in a bowl. Pour the milk over the breadcrumbs and leave for 10 minutes. Squeeze the breadcrumbs dry and add to the meat. Add the garlic, spices, herbs, and salt and pepper to taste and mix well.

Using a piping bag fitted with a large plain nozzle, carefully force the sausage mixture into the casings. Push the mixture evenly along the casing then twist to form sausages.

Cook under a preheated moderate grill or on the barbecue grid, 10 cm (4 inches) above the coals, for 15 to 20 minutes, until golden brown and thoroughly cooked.
Makes about 10 to 12
NOTE: Sausage casings are available from some butchers. They should be soaked overnight in cold water and drained before use.

Spicy Beefburgers; Winchester Sausages

COUNTRY TROUT

2 tablespoons lemon
    or lime juice
1 tablespoon each
    chopped parsley,
    thyme and chives
1 shallot, very finely
    chopped
25 g (1 oz) butter,
    softened
salt and pepper
4 rainbow trout,
    cleaned
4 rashers streaky
    bacon, derinded
4 lemon or lime slices
4 rosemary sprigs

Mix together the lemon or lime juice,
herbs, shallot, butter, and salt and
pepper to taste. Divide the mixture
into 4 portions and spread into the
cavities of the trout. Secure with
cocktail sticks or sew up.

Wrap a rasher of bacon around each
trout. Place each fish on a piece of
foil, top with a lemon or lime slice
and a rosemary sprig and wrap
securely in the foil. Cook under a
preheated moderate grill, or on a
barbecue grid 10 cm (4 inches) above
the coals, for 10 minutes each side.

Serve in the foil, with Barbecued
Potatoes and Chinese Cabbage and
Pepper Salad (see pages 77-78).
Serves 4

Country Trout; Herbed Chicken in Foil

HERBED CHICKEN IN FOIL

2 tablespoons French
    mustard
3 tablespoons natural
    yogurt
6 chicken breasts
salt and pepper
2 tablespoons each
    chopped parsley,
    thyme and chervil
1 tablespoon chopped
    basil
grated rind of ½ lime
    or lemon
juice of 1 lime or
    lemon
lime or lemon slices to
    garnish

Mix the mustard and yogurt together
and use to coat the chicken. Place
each piece of chicken in the centre of a
large piece of lightly oiled foil. Season
well with salt and pepper, scatter a
thick layer of herbs over the top and
sprinkle with the lime or lemon rind
and juice.

Wrap the foil securely around the
chicken. Cook on the barbecue grid,
about 15 cm (6 inches) above the
coals, for 30 to 35 minutes, until
tender. Alternatively, cook in a
preheated moderately hot oven,
190°C (375°F), Gas Mark 5, for
25 minutes.

Serve in the foil, garnished with
lime or lemon slices and accompanied
by French bread.
Serves 6

LEMON CHICKEN

Serve this tasty dish with Sweet and Sour Sauce (below).

8 chicken pieces or
   16 drumsticks
2 lemons
125 g (4 oz) butter
1 clove garlic, crushed
salt and pepper

Make small cuts in the chicken flesh. Brush all over with the juice of one of the lemons. Grate the rind finely and squeeze the juice from the other lemon, then cream together with the butter, garlic, and salt and pepper to taste. Spread a little of the mixture on each piece of chicken and wrap in foil.

Place on the barbecue grid, about 15 cm (6 inches) above the coals, and cook for about 25 minutes. Lower the grid to about 10 cm (4 inches).

Remove the foil from the chicken and place on the lowered grid. Cook for a further 10 to 15 minutes, until the skin is crisp and the chicken is cooked through.
Serves 8

SWEET AND SOUR SAUCE

Prepare this sauce ahead and reheat before serving, with Lemon Chicken (above) or other barbecued meats.

4 tablespoons oil
2 cloves garlic, crushed
2 onions, finely
   chopped
2 green peppers, cored,
   seeded and sliced
4 carrots, thinly sliced
2.5 cm (1 inch) piece
   root ginger, chopped
6 tablespoons white
   wine vinegar
300 ml (½ pint)
   water
50 g (2 oz) demerara
   sugar
2 tablespoons
   cornflour
1 tablespoon soy sauce
salt and pepper

Heat the oil in a frying pan, add the garlic, onions, green peppers, carrots and ginger and fry for about 2 minutes until softened.

Place the remaining ingredients in a bowl, with salt and pepper to taste. Mix thoroughly until smooth, then add to the vegetables. Bring to the boil, stirring, then simmer for 20 minutes until the vegetables are tender and the sauce is thickened.

Serve hot with barbecued meats.
Makes about 900 ml (1½ pints)

Seafood Kebabs

SEAFOOD KEBABS

250 g (8 oz) plaice
   fillets
4 sardines or other
   small fish
8 large cooked
   unshelled prawns
4 scallops, halved
8 rashers streaky
   bacon, derinded
few bay leaves
few lemon wedges
MARINADE:
juice of 1 lemon
4 tablespoons olive oil
1 bouquet garni
salt and pepper
SAUCE:
6 tablespoons
   mayonnaise
1 clove garlic, crushed
1 teaspoon tomato
   purée
dash of Tabasco sauce
1 tablespoon each
   chopped parsley,
   thyme and capers

Cut the plaice into chunks and the sardines into halves.

Mix the marinade ingredients together with salt and pepper to taste, add all the fish and mix well. Leave to marinate for 30 minutes, stirring occasionally.

Put the sauce ingredients in a bowl and mix well. Spoon into a serving dish, cover and set aside.

Drain the marinade from the fish and reserve. Cut the bacon rashers in half and roll up. Arrange the fish alternately on skewers with the bacon, interspersing with bay leaves and lemon wedges to taste. Cook under a preheated moderate grill, or on a barbecue grid 10 cm (4 inches) above the coals, for 5 to 7 minutes on each side, basting with the marinade.

Serve hot, with the sauce.
Serves 8

STUFFED RUMP STEAKS

3 × 500 g (1 lb)
   rump steaks,
   2.5 cm (1 inch)
   thick
120 ml (4 fl oz) red
   wine
4 tablespoons oil
4 tablespoons soy
   sauce
½ teaspoon grated
   nutmeg
75 g (3 oz) butter
2 medium green
   peppers, cored,
   seeded and very
   finely chopped
2 onions, minced
3 celery sticks, very
   finely chopped
250 g (8 oz) fresh
   breadcrumbs
2 tablespoons sweet
   pickle
salt and pepper

Cut off any fat from the steaks then cut a deep pocket in each steak, being careful not to cut through the outside. Place the steaks in a shallow dish, in one layer.

Mix together the wine, oil, soy sauce and nutmeg and sprinkle over the steaks. Leave to marinate for at least 1 hour, turning occasionally.

Melt the butter in a frying pan. Add the green peppers, onions and celery and fry until softened. Remove from the heat and stir in the breadcrumbs, pickle and salt and pepper to taste.

Drain the steaks, reserving the marinade. Carefully spoon the stuffing into the steak pockets and sew the opening with a trussing needle and strong thread.

Place the steaks on the barbecue grid, about 10 cm (4 inches) from the coals. Cook for 10 to 15 minutes on each side, according to taste, basting frequently with the reserved marinade. Cut the steaks in half to serve.
Serves 6

PITTA POCKETS

1 kg (2 lb) sausages
7 pitta breads,
   warmed

Place the sausages on the barbecue grid and cook for about 10 minutes, turning frequently, until well browned all over.

Cut the pitta breads in half and loosen inside with a knife to make a pocket. Place a sausage inside each pocket and spoon in some Sweet and Sour Sauce (see page 75).
Makes 14

BARBECUED LEG OF LAMB

1 × 2.25 kg (5 lb)
   leg of lamb
2 cloves garlic, crushed
150 ml (¼ pint) red
   wine
5 tablespoons olive
   oil
5 tablespoons red
   wine vinegar
4 tablespoons
   chopped parsley
1 teaspoon mixed
   dried herbs
salt and pepper
small bunch of
   parsley

Bone the leg of lamb, without cutting all the way through, so that the meat can be opened flat.

Mix together the garlic, wine, oil, vinegar, chopped parsley, herbs and salt and pepper to taste. Lay the lamb on the barbecue grid, fat side up, about 15 cm (6 inches) above the coals. Baste with the wine mixture, using the bunch of parsley as the basting brush, and cook for 50 to 60 minutes or until the lamb is cooked through, turning occasionally and basting frequently.
Serves 6

MARINATED REDCURRANT CHICKEN

75 g (3 oz)
   redcurrant jelly
4 tablespoons lemon
   juice
4 tablespoons oil
4 tablespoons chicken
   stock
½ teaspoon dry
   mustard
½ teaspoon
   Worcestershire
   sauce
salt and pepper
4 or 8 chicken pieces

Melt the jelly in a saucepan. Stir in the lemon juice, oil, stock, mustard, Worcestershire sauce and salt and pepper to taste.

Arrange the chicken pieces in a shallow dish, in one layer, and pour over the jelly mixture. Cover and leave to marinate overnight.

Drain the chicken pieces, reserving the marinade, and place on the barbecue grid, about 15 cm (6 inches) above the coals. Cook for about 50 minutes or until the chicken is cooked through, turning frequently and basting with the reserved marinade.
Serves 4

SERVING QUANTITIES

Barbecues can be anything from a small family gathering to a larger buffet-style party. For this reason the serving quantities vary throughout this chapter. When menu-planning, increase or decrease the recipe ingredients in proportion, depending on the number and type of guests you are catering for.

SWEETCORN SALAD

2 × 326 g (11½ oz) cans sweetcorn
2 sticks celery
4 tomatoes
4 spring onions
4 tablespoons mayonnaise
1 tablespoon French mustard

Drain the sweetcorn and place in a serving bowl. Chop the celery, tomatoes and spring onions finely and add to the bowl with the remaining ingredients. Toss thoroughly to serve.
Serves 12

BARBECUED POTATOES

12 medium potatoes
oil for brushing
salt
butter to serve

Brush the potato skins with oil and sprinkle with salt. Slit each potato down one side.

If space on the barbecue is limited, bake the potatoes in a preheated moderately hot oven, 200°C (400°F), Gas Mark 6, for 45 minutes. Place the potatoes in the hot charcoal for a further 10 minutes.

If you have room on the barbecue, wrap potatoes in a double thickness of foil and cook in the charcoal for about 45 minutes, turning occasionally. Serve with butter.
Serves 12

BARBECUED DRUMSTICKS

12 chicken drumsticks
HONEY AND ORANGE SAUCE:
2 tablespoons clear honey
1 tablespoon Worcester-shire sauce
grated rind and juice of ½ orange
1 tablespoon tomato purée
1 tablespoon soy sauce

Mix the sauce ingredients together in a small basin and use to brush all over the drumsticks. Place them all on a large piece of foil and fold over to enclose completely. Leave to marinate for 1 hour.

Remove the foil, place the chicken on the barbecue grid and cook for 15 to 20 minutes, turning frequently and basting with the remaining sauce, until the skin is crisp. Serve with Sweet and Sour Sauce (see page 75).
Serves 12

Sweetcorn Salad; Barbecued Potatoes; Barbecued Drumsticks

SPICED RICE SALAD

75 g (3 oz) dried
    apricots, chopped
125 g (4 oz) long-
    grain rice
salt
1 tablespoon corn oil
50 g (2 oz) split
    almonds
1 teaspoon grated
    nutmeg
3 celery sticks, diced
4 spring onions,
    sliced
1 tablespoon chopped
    coriander
4 tablespoons French
    dressing (see page
    151)

Cover the apricots with boiling water, leave to soak for 1 hour, then drain well.

Place the rice in a pan of boiling salted water and simmer for 12 to 15 minutes, until tender. Rinse thoroughly, drain and leave to cool slightly.

Heat the oil in a small pan, add the almonds and fry until pale golden. Add the nutmeg and fry for a few seconds.

Place the warm rice in a salad bowl with the apricots. Add the spiced almonds with their oil. Mix in the celery, spring onions and coriander. Pour the dressing over the salad and toss thoroughly before serving.
Serves 4
VARIATION: Use stoned and chopped dates instead of the dried apricots; these will not require pre-soaking.

CURRIED POTATO SALAD

750 g (1½ lb) waxy
    potatoes, peeled
salt
6 tablespoons
    Mayonnaise (see
    page 152)
1 teaspoon curry
    paste
1 tablespoon tomato
    ketchup
4 tablespoons natural
    yogurt
1 small onion, finely
    chopped
1 small green pepper,
    cored, seeded and
    chopped

Cook the potatoes in boiling salted water until tender. Drain well, chop roughly and leave to cool in a mixing bowl.

Mix together the mayonnaise, curry paste, tomato ketchup and yogurt, then pour over the potatoes. Add the onion and green pepper and toss well until coated. Transfer to a serving dish.
Serves 6

CALIFORNIAN COLESLAW

1 dessert apple, cored
4 tablespoons Honey
    and lemon dressing
    (see page 151)
2 oranges
125 g (4 oz) each
    white and black
    grapes, halved and
    seeded
250 g (8 oz) white
    cabbage, finely
    shredded
2 tablespoons
    chopped chives
2 tablespoons roasted
    sunflower seeds

Slice the apple thinly into the dressing and toss until thoroughly coated.

Remove the peel and pith from the oranges, break into segments and add to the bowl.

Add the remaining ingredients and toss well. Transfer to a salad bowl.
Serves 6 to 8

RED SALAD

250 g (8 oz) red
    cabbage
5 tablespoons Garlic
    dressing (see page
    151)
1 head of radicchio
1 small red onion
1 bunch of radishes

Finely shred the cabbage and place in a bowl with the dressing. Toss well and leave for 1 hour.

Separate the radicchio into leaves, then tear into pieces; thinly slice the onion and radishes. Add to the bowl and toss thoroughly, then transfer to a salad bowl.
Serves 6 to 8

CHINESE CABBAGE AND PEPPER SALAD

1 leek, finely sliced
1 Chinese cabbage,
    shredded
1 green pepper,
    cored, seeded and
    finely sliced
6 tablespoons Herb
    dressing (see page
    152)

Separate the leek slices into rings and mix with the Chinese cabbage in a bowl. Add the green pepper and dressing and toss thoroughly. Transfer to a salad bowl and serve immediately.
Serves 6 to 8

Californian Coleslaw; Red Salad; Curried Potato Salad

APPLE AMBER

PASTRY:
75 g (3 oz) butter or margarine
175 g (6 oz) plain flour, sifted
1-2 tablespoons iced water

FILLING:
25 g (1 oz) butter
500 g (1 lb) cooking apples, peeled, cored and sliced
175 g (6 oz) caster sugar
1 teaspoon ground cinnamon
2 eggs, separated

Rub the butter or margarine into the flour until the mixture resembles fine breadcrumbs. Add enough water to form a firm dough.

Knead lightly on a floured surface and roll out thinly. Use to line a 20 cm (8 inch) fluted flan ring. Line with greaseproof paper and dried beans and bake for 15 minutes. Remove the paper and beans and return to the oven for 5 minutes. Remove the flan ring and cool on a wire rack.

Melt the butter in a pan and add the apples. Cover and cook over low heat until pulped. Beat in 75 g (3 oz) sugar, the cinnamon and egg yolks.

Pour into a flan case and bake in a preheated moderate oven, 180°C (350°F), Gas Mark 4, for 15 minutes. Lower the oven temperature to 140°C (275°F), Gas Mark 1.

Whisk the egg whites stiffly, then whisk in half the remaining sugar. Fold in the rest and pile the meringue over the apple. Return to the oven for 1 hour or until meringue is crisp. Serve warm or cold with single cream.
Serves 6

FLUFFY LEMON TRIFLE

1 packet trifle sponge cakes
3 lemons
3 eggs, separated
1 × 397 g (14 oz) can condensed milk

TO DECORATE:
142 ml (5 fl oz) double or whipping cream, whipped
25 g (1 oz) flaked almonds, toasted

Crumble the cakes into a large dish. Grate the rind from one of the lemons and squeeze the juice from all of them.

Beat the egg yolks with the condensed milk, lemon rind and juice until thick and pale. Moisten the cake in the dish with 8 tablespoons of the mixture.

Whisk the egg whites until stiff and fold into the remaining lemon mixture. Pour over the sponge cakes and smooth the surface. Decorate with piped cream and flaked almonds. Chill in the refrigerator until serving time.
Serves 10

GOOSEBERRY GINGER CRUNCH

8 gingernuts, crushed
25 g (1 oz) butter, melted
500 g (1 lb) gooseberries
1 tablespoon water
125 g (4 oz) caster sugar
1 egg white, stiffly whisked
284 ml (10 fl oz) double cream
few drops of green food colouring

Combine the gingernut crumbs and butter and leave on one side.

Place the gooseberries and water in a pan, cover and simmer for 15 minutes, until the fruit has pulped. Sieve or work in an electric blender until smooth. Stir in the sugar and leave to cool.

Fold the egg white into the gooseberry purée with the whipped cream and food colouring.

Divide half this mixture between glass serving dishes and sprinkle over half the gingernut mixture; repeat these layers. Chill well before serving.
Serves 6

FRUIT MERINGUE BASKETS

4 egg whites
250 g (8 oz) caster sugar
284 ml (10 fl oz) whipping cream
50 g (2 oz) icing sugar
1 tablespoon liqueur (optional)
750 g (1½ lb) fresh or frozen and thawed soft fruit (e.g. raspberries, strawberries, cherries)

Mark six 10 cm (4 inch) circles on silicone paper. Place on oiled baking sheets and brush the paper with oil.

Whisk the egg whites until stiff. Add half the sugar and continue whisking until the mixture is smooth. Fold in the remaining sugar. Spread two-thirds of the meringue over the circles to form bases. Pipe the rest around the edges to make rims.

Bake in a preheated very cool oven, 120°C (250°F), Gas Mark ½, for 2 hours, until dry and crisp. Remove the paper and cool on a wire rack.

Whip the cream with the icing sugar and liqueur, if using. Fold in the fruit, reserving a few pieces. Pile into the baskets and decorate with reserved fruit.
Serves 6

Gooseberry Ginger Crunch; Apple Amber; Fruit Meringue Baskets

NUTTY APPLE PIES

1 kg (2 lb) cooking
  apples, peeled,
  cored and thinly
  sliced
50 g (2 oz) brown
  sugar
3/4 teaspoon ground
  cinnamon
1/4 teaspoon grated
  nutmeg
125 g (4 oz)
  walnuts, finely
  chopped
SWEETCRUST
  PASTRY:
175 g (6 oz) plain
  flour
50 g (2 oz)
  granulated sugar
1/2 teaspoon salt
125 g (4 oz) butter
1 egg yolk

Mix together the apples, brown sugar, spices and half the walnuts. Divide between 6 individual baking dishes, about 10 cm (4 inches) in diameter and about 4 cm (1¾ inches) deep.

To make the pastry, mix together the flour, granulated sugar and salt and rub in the butter until the mixture resembles breadcrumbs. Stir in the egg yolk and the remaining nuts. If necessary, add a little water to bind the dough together.

Divide the dough into 6 portions and pat each one into a round about 15 cm (6 inches) in diameter. Place the dough rounds on the baking dishes and pinch over the edges to seal. Make a few slits in the top of each one.

Bake in a preheated moderate oven, 180°C (350°F), Gas Mark 4, for 40 to 45 minutes or until the crust is golden. Serve warm or cold.
Makes 6

SPICY FRUIT KEBABS

2 oranges
2 red-skinned apples
2 bananas
16 pineapple chunks,
  fresh or canned
125 g (4 oz) butter
2 tablespoons sugar
1 teaspoon ground
  allspice or
  coriander

Cut each orange into 4 thick slices and halve each slice. Core the apples and cut each into 4 wedges. Cut each banana into 4 thick slices. Thread 2 orange pieces, 1 apple wedge, 1 banana slice and 2 pineapple chunks onto each of 8 skewers.

Melt the butter in a saucepan on the side of the barbecue. Stir in the sugar and spice.

Place the fruit kebabs on the barbecue grid, about 15 cm (6 inches) above the coals. Brush with the spice butter and cook for about 5 minutes, basting frequently and turning to brown on all sides.
Serves 8

Nutty Apple Pies; Spicy Fruit Kebabs

APPLE STREUSEL PIE

250 g (8 oz) plain
  flour
125 g (4 oz) butter
1 tablespoon icing
  sugar
1 egg yolk
2 tablespoons cold
  water
FILLING:
1 kg (2 lb) cooking
  apples, peeled,
  cored and sliced
50 g (2 oz) raisins
125 g (4 oz) plain
  flour
125 g (4 oz) caster
  sugar
50 g (2 oz) butter
284 ml (10 fl oz)
  double cream
TOPPING:
50 g (2 oz) caster
  sugar
2 teaspoons cinnamon

Sift the flour into a bowl and rub in the butter until the mixture resembles breadcrumbs. Stir in the icing sugar and bind together with the egg yolk and water. Roll out the pastry thinly and use to line two 18 cm (7 inch) or one 25 cm (10 inch) flan tins.

To make the filling, mix the apples and raisins together. Sift the flour into a bowl and stir in the sugar. Rub in the butter, using the fingertips. Spoon half the rubbed-in mixture into the flan. Cover with the apples and raisins, then pour over the cream. Spoon over the remaining rubbed-in mixture and sprinkle with the topping.

Bake in a preheated moderately hot oven, 200°C (400°F), Gas Mark 6, for 25 minutes, then reduce the heat to 190°C (375°F), Gas Mark 5, and cook for a further 10 minutes. Serve hot or cold.
Serves 8

Spiced Bananas; Toasted Marshmallows

BAKED BANANAS

12 slightly under-ripe
  bananas

Bury the bananas, in their skins, in the charcoal embers just outside the hottest part of the fire. Leave for about 5 minutes, until the skins are charred. Remove with tongs.
Serve in a napkin.
Serves 12

SPICED BANANAS

8 bananas, peeled
2 tablespoons lemon
  juice
8 tablespoons soft
  brown sugar
50 g (2 oz) butter
1 teaspoon
  cinnamon

Place each banana on a double piece of foil. Brush well with the lemon juice and sprinkle 1 tablespoon sugar on each. Cream together the butter and cinnamon and divide between the bananas, dotting along the top.

Wrap each banana securely and cook on the barbecue grid, about 10 cm (4 inches) above the coals, for 10 minutes. Unwrap and serve hot.
Serves 8

DESSERTS FOR BARBECUES

There is no doubt that fresh air sharpens appetites so make sure you have a good selection and quantity of desserts.

Most fruit desserts like Baked Bananas (above) and Spicy Fruit Kebabs (opposite) do not need much cooking, so they can usually be done after the main cooking when temperatures are lower, or if wrapped in foil they can be cooked at the edge of the barbecue at the same time.

Mix and match with a few chilled desserts like Fluffy Lemon Trifle (page 80) or Fruit Meringue Baskets (page 80).

TOASTED MARSHMALLOWS

An ideal treat to include in your barbecue for children.

2 packets
  marshmallows

Spear one marshmallow at a time onto a kebab skewer or clean stick. Hold over the barbecue, turning frequently, until puffed up and golden. Serve immediately.
Serves 8

CLARET CUP

1 measure maraschino
2 measures orange
   Curaçao
2 tablespoons caster
   sugar
1.2 litres (2 pints)
   Claret

Put the ingredients into a large bowl. Add ice and stir until the sugar is dissolved. Decorate with fruits in season.
Serves 4 to 6

PEACH CUP

2 ripe peaches
1.5 litres (2½ pints)
   still Moselle,
   chilled
3 tablespoons caster
   sugar
750 ml (1¼ pints)
   sparkling Moselle,
   chilled

Peel and chop the peaches into a large bowl. Pour one bottle of still Moselle over the fruit. Add the sugar, stir gently, cover and leave for 30 minutes. Add the second bottle of still Moselle.
   Just before serving, add the sparkling Moselle.
Serves 8 to 10
NOTE: This cup must be served chilled but no ice should be put in the drink.

RHINE WINE CUP

2 measures
   maraschino
1 measure orange
   Curaçao
1½ teaspoons caster
   sugar
1.2 litres (2 pints)
   white wine

Place the ingredients in a large jug or bowl. Add a few pieces of ice and stir well. Decorate with fruits in season.
Serves 4 to 6

COCKTAILS FOR BARBECUES

There can be few better ways to get a barbecue party off to a good start than by serving a few cleverly-concocted cocktails. They invite comment, stimulate conversation and warm the spirits for al fresco treats to come.

   It is important to measure ingredients accurately to get the proportions right. A 'measure' in the recipes here refers to a standard measure of 45 ml (1½ fl oz or 3 tablespoons) or a 'jigger' – and is worth buying if you serve cocktails regularly. To improvise, use a standard liqueur glass which holds about 30 ml (1 fl oz or 2 tablespoons) and adapt accordingly.

CLARET PUNCH

250 g (8 oz) caster
  sugar
3.5 litres (6 pints)
  Claret
2.25 litres (4 pints)
  sparkling mineral
  water
300 ml (½ pint)
  lemon juice
2 measures orange
  Curaçao

Place the ingredients in a large punch bowl containing plenty of ice. Stir gently until the sugar is dissolved. Decorate with slices of fruits in season. Keep the punch bowl packed with ice.
Serves 20 to 25

SAUTERNE PUNCH

250 g (8 oz) caster
  sugar
2.25 litres (4 pints)
  Sauterne
1 measure maraschino
1 measure orange
  Curaçao
1 measure Grand
  Marnier

Dissolve the sugar in the wine in a large jug, then pour over a large quantity of ice in a punch bowl and stir in the remaining ingredients. Add slices of fruits in season.
Serves 10 to 15
NOTE: Any other medium sweet white wine can be used in place of Sauterne.

CHAMPAGNE PUNCH

250 g (8 oz) caster
  sugar
2.25 litres (4 pints)
  Champagne
1.2 litres (2 pints)
  sparkling mineral
  water
2 measures brandy
2 measures
  maraschino
2 measures orange
  Curaçao

Put the ingredients into a large punch bowl containing plenty of ice cubes and stir until the sugar is dissolved. Add slices of fruits in season.
Serves 15 to 20

OPPOSITE: *Claret Cup; Peach Cup; Rhine Wine Cup*
RIGHT: *Claret Punch; Sauterne Punch*

BUFFET PARTIES

Buffet parties are the entertaining occasions favoured by busy people who have little help. They are infinitely popular with those who dislike formality and certainly prove welcome, fraught-free parties for parents with young children who have not yet mastered the rigours of polite and tidy table manners.

Wonderfully relaxed, they are the 'almost anything goes' type of occasion and food can either be deliciously simple or sumptuously extravagant depending upon your pocket and available time. Occasions such as these do not stand on formality and can take place late morning as a buffet brunch/breakfast, at mid-day as a buffet lunch or after the theatre as a buffet supper.

The chief advantages of such parties is that they prove a very agreeable form of entertaining fairly large numbers, guests help themselves to food, and single people enjoy them since there is no inevitable 'pairing off' as with dinner parties.

Most of the preparation for such parties can be done well in advance, allowing you to enjoy the party spirits too. Good planning is still a must, but once plentiful supplies of plates, napkins, glasses, cutlery and food have been laid out there is little more to do than occasionally check in case anything runs low.

A few items of equipment prove useful aids to buffet party cooks – a stay-hot plate for keeping food warm is useful if you plan to serve hot main course dishes; lots of rigid salad boxes are an enormous help in keeping salads fresh for up to 24 hours in the refrigerator; and a large drinks cooler that will take ice and a few bottles of wine will help to keep everything flowing smoothly.

MUSHROOMS ITALIENNE

8 shelled scallops
8 tablespoons dry
  white wine
2 parsley sprigs
½ small onion
strip of lemon rind
250 g (8 oz) peeled
  prawns
500 g (1 lb) button
  mushrooms, thinly
  sliced
175 ml (6 fl oz) olive oil
4 tablespoons lemon
  or lime juice
1 clove garlic, crushed
2 teaspoons chopped
  parsley
salt and pepper
few lettuce leaves
TO GARNISH:
parsley sprigs
lime or lemon slices

Separate the coral from the white scallop meat then slice the scallops.

Put the wine, parsley sprigs, onion and lemon rind into a pan, add the scallops and cook for 2 minutes.

Using a slotted spoon, lift out the fish and put into a bowl. Leave to cool, then stir in the prawns.

Put the mushrooms into another bowl and pour over the oil and lemon or lime juice. Sprinkle with the garlic, parsley and plenty of pepper. Toss well and leave to stand for 30 minutes. Stir in a little salt, add to the fish and stir well.

Arrange the lettuce leaves on individual serving dishes and pile the mushroom mixture on top. Cover and chill until required.

Garnish with parsley and lime or lemon slices to serve.

Serves 8 to 12

CRISPY CHEESE FRIES

125 g (4 oz) butter
125 g (4 oz) plain
  flour
900 ml (1½ pints)
  milk
salt and pepper
freshly grated nutmeg
350 g (12 oz) Gruyère
  cheese, grated
4 tablespoons grated
  Parmesan cheese
2 × 177 g (6 oz) can
  crabmeat, drained
  and flaked
4 egg yolks, beaten
2 eggs
4 tablespoons milk
fresh breadcrumbs for
  coating
oil for deep-frying
fried parsley sprigs to
  garnish

Melt the butter in a pan, stir in the flour and cook for 2 minutes. Gradually add the milk, stirring constantly. Bring to the boil, and add salt, pepper and nutmeg to taste. Add the cheeses and stir until melted.

Remove from the heat and mix in the crabmeat and egg yolks. Spread the mixture in a shallow baking tin to a 1 cm (½ inch) thickness. Cover with foil and chill for 3 to 4 hours.

Cut the paste into rectangles, about 4 cm (1½ inches) long. Beat the egg with the milk. Dip the cheese cubes into the egg mixture, then into the breadcrumbs to coat evenly. Heat the oil in a deep-fryer to 190°C (375°F) and fry the cheese cubes in batches until crisp and golden. Keep hot in the oven until ready to serve. Garnish with the parsley before serving.

Serves 12

ARDENNES PÂTÉ

500 g (1 lb) pork fillet, diced
500 g (1 lb) belly pork, diced
500 g (1 lb) minced veal
750 g (1½ lb) chicken livers, chopped
8 tablespoons brandy
4 teaspoons chopped thyme
2 tablespoons green peppercorns
salt and pepper
8-12 rashers streaky bacon, derinded
TO GARNISH:
thyme sprigs
lemon slices

Combine the pork, veal and chicken livers in a large bowl. Stir in the brandy, thyme, peppercorns, and salt and pepper to taste. Cover and chill for 2 hours.

Spoon the mixture into a lightly greased 1 kg (2 lb) loaf tin. Stretch the bacon and use to cover the pâté. Cover with foil and place in a roasting pan. Pour in enough boiling water to come halfway up the sides of the pan. Cook in a preheated moderate oven, 180°C (350°F), Gas Mark 4, for 1½ hours.

Leave to cool in the tin; turn out when cold. Garnish with thyme and lemon slices, and serve with toast.
Serves 16

CHICKEN LIVER PÂTÉ

125 g (4 oz) butter
250 g (8 oz) back bacon, derinded and chopped
4 cloves garlic, crushed
2 small onions, chopped
1 kg (2 lb) chicken livers, chopped
salt and pepper
4 thyme sprigs
4 parsley sprigs
250 g (8 oz) button mushrooms, chopped
120 ml (4 fl oz) dry sherry
120 ml (4 fl oz) double cream
2 teaspoons lemon juice
watercress sprigs

Melt the butter in a large pan, add the bacon, garlic and onion and cook gently for 3 minutes. Stir in the chicken livers and cook for 5 minutes. Season liberally with salt and pepper. Stir in the herbs and mushrooms. Add the sherry and cook until the liquid has evaporated. Cool, then work in an electric blender until smooth. Stir in the cream and lemon juice.

Spoon into a greased ovenproof dish. Cover with a lid and stand in a roasting pan, containing water to a depth of 2.5 cm (1 inch). Bake in a preheated cool oven, 150°C (300°F), Gas Mark 2, for 2 to 2½ hours, until cooked through. Allow to cool. Cover and chill until required.

Garnish with watercress and serve with hot buttered toast.
Serves 12

OPPOSITE: *Mushrooms Italienne; Crispy Cheese Fries*
RIGHT: *Ardennes Pâté; Chicken Liver Pâté*

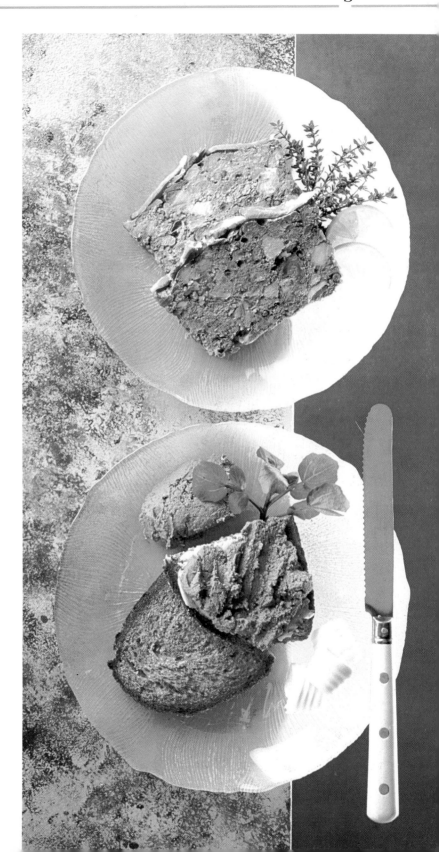

BARBECUE DIP

6 spring onions
1 green pepper
250 g (8 oz) red
    Cheddar cheese
300 g (10 oz) natural
    yogurt
2 tablespoons tomato
    ketchup
2 tablespoons
    mayonnaise
1 teaspoon
    Worcestershire
    sauce
Tabasco sauce
salt and pepper
TO GARNISH:
paprika or chopped
    chives

Finely chop the spring onions and green pepper, discarding the core and seeds. Grate the cheese, using a fine grater.

Combine all the dip ingredients in a large bowl adding Tabasco, salt and pepper to taste; mix well. Spoon into a serving dish and chill.

Sprinkle with paprika or chives. Serve with a selection of savoury biscuits and raw vegetables, such as red and green pepper, carrot, celery, cucumber and cauliflower florets.
Serves 12

FRUITY CHEESE DIP

2 × 227 g (8 oz) cartons
    cottage cheese
    with pineapple
125 g (4 oz)
    Leicester cheese,
    finely grated
120 ml (4 fl oz) double
    cream, whipped
finely grated rind of
    2 oranges
175 g (6 oz) green
    grapes, seeded and
    chopped
2 celery sticks, chopped
celery salt
salt and pepper
parsley sprig to
    garnish

Place the cheeses and cream in a bowl and mix well. Stir in the orange rind, grapes and celery. Add celery salt, salt and pepper to taste. Pile into a serving bowl and chill.

Garnish with parsley and serve with a selection of the following: crisps, savoury biscuits, cubes of French bread, Melba toast, raw carrot, celery, cucumber, cauliflower florets, radishes.
Serves 12

LEICESTER KIPPER PÂTÉ

500 g (1 lb) kipper
    fillets, skin
    removed
2 tablespoons lemon
    juice
120 ml (4 fl oz) milk
150 ml (5 oz) natural
    low-fat yogurt
175 g (6 oz) Leicester
    cheese, grated
pepper
TO GARNISH:
parsley sprigs
lemon slices

Poach the kippers in the lemon juice
and milk for 10 minutes. Drain,
reserving the liquor. Place the fish in
a bowl and mash until smooth. Blend
in the yogurt, cheese and sufficient
liquor to give a smooth consistency.
Add pepper to taste and spoon into
small dishes. Chill until required.
    Garnish with parsley and lemon
slices and serve with Melba toast.
Serves 8

SARDINE FISH CREAM

226 g (8 oz)
    medium-fat curd
    cheese
2 × 120 g (4¼ oz)
    cans sardines in
    tomato sauce
4 teaspoons chopped
    chives
4 spring onions,
    finely chopped
6 drops
    Worcestershire
    sauce
2 teaspoons lemon
    juice
salt and pepper
chopped chives to
    garnish

Place the cheese and sardines with
their juice in a bowl and mash
together. Add the chives, spring
onions, Worcestershire sauce, lemon
juice and salt and pepper to taste. Mix
well.
    Spoon the sardine mixture into a
small serving bowl and garnish with
chives. Serve with wholemeal bread
or crispbread.
Serves 8

BOURSIN-STUFFED EGGS

8 hard-boiled eggs
125 g (4 oz) Boursin
    cheese with garlic
6 tablespoons single
    cream
25 g (1 oz) walnuts,
    finely chopped
salt and pepper
1 lettuce, shredded
paprika to garnish

Cut the eggs in half lengthways and
remove the yolks. Place in a bowl
with the Boursin and cream and
blend well. Add the walnuts, and
salt and pepper to taste. Spoon or pipe
the mixture into the egg white
halves.
    Arrange the lettuce on a serving
plate, place the eggs on top and
sprinkle with paprika. Serve with
brown bread and butter.
Serves 8

OPPOSITE: *Barbecue Dip; Fruity Cheese Dip*
RIGHT: *Leicester Kipper Pâté; Sardine Fish Cream;*
Boursin-stuffed Eggs

Guacamole with Crudités

SKORDALIA

SAUCE:
8 egg yolks
12 fat cloves garlic, crushed
600 ml (1 pint) olive oil
250 g (8 oz) ground almonds
250 g (8 oz) fresh breadcrumbs
2 tablespoons lemon juice
2 tablespoons chopped parsley
TO SERVE:
1 kg (2 lb) small courgettes
1 kg (2 lb) French beans
1 large cauliflower
salt
1 kg (2 lb) tomatoes
15 eggs, hard-boiled

Put 4 egg yolks and 6 garlic cloves in an electric blender or food processor. Switch on at full speed and trickle in half the oil slowly until the mixture is thick. Pour into a large bowl.

Repeat this process with the remaining egg yolks, garlic and olive oil, then add to the bowl. Add the remaining ingredients and mix together thoroughly. Divide between 2 serving bowls.

Top and tail the courgettes and beans. Break the cauliflower into florets. Cook the vegetables separately in boiling salted water for a few minutes until just tender but still firm. Drain and leave to cool.

Cut the courgettes lengthways into sticks, tomatoes into quarters, and the eggs in half lengthways.

Place the bowls of skordalia on large platters and arrange the eggs and vegetables around them to serve.
Serves 30

GUACAMOLE WITH CRUDITÉS

4 ripe avocado pears
juice of 1 lemon
4 tomatoes
1 small onion, grated
2 cloves garlic, crushed
1 teaspoon Worcestershire sauce
120 ml (4 oz) natural yogurt
salt and pepper
1 small cauliflower
8 carrots
8 celery sticks
1 cucumber
4 green or red peppers

Halve the avocados and remove the stones. Scoop the flesh into a bowl and mash with the lemon juice. Skin, seed and chop the tomatoes and add to the bowl with the onion, garlic, Worcestershire sauce, yogurt, and salt and pepper to taste. Beat thoroughly until smooth and divide between 2 serving dishes.

Break the cauliflower into florets and cut the remaining vegetables into matchstick pieces, discarding the core and seeds from the peppers.

Place each dish on a large plate and surround with the vegetables.
Serves 8 to 10

VICHYSSOISE

75 g (3 oz) butter
350 g (12 oz) onions, chopped
1.5 kg (3 lb) leeks, sliced
750 g (1½ lb) potatoes, sliced
3.5 litres (6 pints) chicken stock
284 ml (10 fl oz) single cream
salt and pepper
chopped chives or spring onion tops to garnish

Melt the butter in a large pan, add the onions and fry gently until translucent but not browned. Add the leeks and fry for 5 minutes. Add the potatoes and stock. Bring to the boil, cover and simmer for 30 minutes.

Cool slightly, then sieve or work in an electric blender until smooth. Transfer to a large bowl or soup tureen, stir in the cream and season with salt and pepper to taste. Chill.

Sprinkle with chopped chives or spring onion tops to serve. Follow with Gammon with Cumberland Sauce (see page 95).
Serves 20
(Illustrated on page 95)

OPPOSITE: *French Tomato Tartlets; Ratatouille Tartlets*

FRENCH TOMATO TARTLETS

SHORTCRUST
   PASTRY:
*500 g (1 lb) plain
   flour*
pinch of salt
125 g (4 oz) lard
125 g (4 oz) butter
*50 g (2 oz) grated
   Parmesan cheese*
*3-4 tablespoons iced
   water*
FILLING:
50 g (2 oz) butter
4 onions, sliced
*750 g (1½ lb)
   tomatoes, skinned
   and thickly sliced*
*24 anchovy fillets,
   soaked in a little
   milk for 10 minutes
   then drained*
48 black olives
3-4 tablespoons oil

To make the pastry, sift the flour and salt into a mixing bowl, then rub in the lard and butter until the mixture resembles fine breadcrumbs. Stir in the cheese, then mix in sufficient water to make a firm dough. Cover and chill for 15 minutes. Knead lightly, roll out on a floured board and use to line twelve 7.5 cm (3 inch) individual flan tins. Prick the base of each case. Chill for 30 minutes.

Melt the butter in a pan, add the onions and cook until lightly browned. Cool, then sprinkle over the base of the pastry cases. Place the tomatoes on top, then arrange 2 anchovy fillets in a cross on top and place an olive in each quarter. Sprinkle a little oil over each tart.

Bake in a preheated moderate oven, 180°C (350°F), Gas Mark 4, for 25 to 30 minutes, until the pastry is golden.

Serve hot or cold.
Serves 12

RATATOUILLE TARTLETS

SHORTCRUST
   PASTRY:
*500 g (1 lb) plain
   flour*
pinch of salt
125 g (4 oz) lard
125 g (4 oz) butter
*3-4 tablespoons iced
   water*
RATATOUILLE:
25 g (1 oz) butter
2 cloves garlic, sliced
2 onions, sliced
*2 small aubergines,
   chopped*
2 courgettes, sliced
*8 tomatoes, skinned,
   seeded and chopped*
*2 tablespoons tomato
   purée*
salt and pepper
TO SERVE:
*Parmesan cheese
   (optional)*

Make the pastry and chill as for French Tomato Tartlets (see left), omitting the cheese. Knead lightly, then roll out on a floured board and use to line twelve 7.5 cm (3 inch) individual flan tins. Prick the bases. Chill for 30 minutes.

Melt the butter in a pan, add the garlic and onions and cook gently for 10 minutes. Stir in the aubergines, courgettes, tomatoes, tomato purée, and salt and pepper to taste. Cover and simmer for 20 minutes.

Line the pastry cases with foil or greaseproof paper and beans and bake in a preheated moderately hot oven, 200°C (400°F), Gas Mark 6, for 12 minutes, until golden brown. Remove the paper and beans and cook for a further 5 minutes.

Spoon the ratatouille into the flan cases and sprinkle with Parmesan if liked. Serve hot or cold.
Serves 12

CRUNCHY DRUMSTICKS

125 g (4 oz) fresh
   white breadcrumbs
2 tablespoons each
   chopped parsley
   and chives
2 tablespoons grated
   Parmesan cheese
4 tablespoons
   blanched almonds,
   chopped
16 chicken drumsticks
salt and pepper
2 eggs, beaten
125 g (4 oz) butter
4 cloves garlic,
   crushed

Mix the breadcrumbs, parsley, chives, cheese and almonds together. Season the drumsticks with salt and pepper, dip into the beaten egg and coat with the breadcrumb mixture.

Melt the butter in a pan, add the garlic and cook for 1 minute, without browning.

Place the drumsticks in a large roasting pan, spoon over the garlic butter and cook in a preheated moderate oven, 180°C (350°F), Gas Mark 4, for 35 to 40 minutes, basting occasionally, until well cooked and golden brown. Serve hot or cold.
Makes 16

CIRCASSIAN CHICKEN

5 × 1.5 kg (3½ lb)
   chickens
5 carrots
5 onions, quartered
5 bouquet garni
salt and pepper
175 g (6 oz)
   hazelnuts
250 g (8 oz) walnut
   pieces
175 g (6 oz) butter
500 g (1 lb) onions,
   sliced
175 g (6 oz) ground
   almonds
1 kg (2.2 lb) carton
   natural low-fat
   yogurt
1 teaspoon paprika
watercress sprigs to
   garnish

Place each chicken in a pan with a carrot, onion, bouquet garni and salt and pepper to taste. Cover with cold water, bring to the boil, then simmer for 1½ hours. Leave in the cooking liquid until cool, then remove the skin and cut all flesh from the bones into pieces; set aside. Reserve 300 ml (½ pint) of the cooking liquid.

Grind the hazelnuts and 175 g (6 oz) of the walnuts; set aside.

Melt the butter in a large pan, add the remaining walnut pieces and fry until golden brown. Remove with a slotted spoon and set aside for garnish. Add the sliced onions to the pan and fry until soft but not brown.

Add the ground hazelnuts and walnuts to the pan with the ground almonds, yogurt, paprika and reserved stock. Add the chicken meat and heat through gently, stirring.

Transfer to a warmed serving dish, and garnish with the walnuts and watercress. Serve with Tomato and Cucumber Salad (see page 106) and Pilaff (see page 107).
Serves 30

GAMMON WITH CUMBERLAND SAUCE

1 gammon, on the bone, weighing about 4.5 kg (10 lb)
4 bay leaves
1 tablespoon black peppercorns
1 onion
8 cloves
175 g (6 oz) dried breadcrumbs
SAUCE:
2 oranges
2 lemons
1 × 454 g (1 lb) jar redcurrant jelly
150 ml (¼ pint) port
TO GARNISH:
1 orange, sliced and twisted
watercress sprigs

Place the gammon in a large pan with the bay leaves, peppercorns and onion studded with the cloves. Cover with cold water, bring to the boil and skim the surface. Simmer for about 3½ hours, allowing 20 minutes per 500 g (1 lb) plus 20 minutes over. Leave to cool in the cooking liquid.

Meanwhile prepare the sauce. Peel the rind thinly from the oranges and lemons and cut into fine shreds. Cover with cold water, bring to the boil and boil for 2 minutes; drain.

Squeeze the juice from the fruit, place in a pan with the redcurrant jelly and heat gently, stirring, until the jelly melts. Simmer for 5 minutes, then add the port and shredded rind. Leave to cool.

Remove skin from the gammon and press the breadcrumbs into the fat. Carve and arrange on a serving platter. Garnish with orange twists and watercress. Serve with the sauce.
Serves 20
NOTE: Vichyssoise (see page 92) is an ideal soup to serve before this dish.

PREPARING IN ADVANCE

Cooked rice and pasta are popular and ideal accompaniments to serve with main meal dishes for buffet parties but can be costly on last minute attention.

It is possible to freeze cooked pasta and rice and then to reheat it so that it still retains that slight freshly-cooked bite.

Cook rice and pasta according to packet instructions reducing the cooking times by about 3 minutes. Drain, cool quickly and freeze in rigid containers for up to 3 months.

To cook, add the frozen rice and pasta to rapidly boiling, slightly salted water and bring quickly to the boil again. Cook for 2-3 minutes, drain and serve.

OPPOSITE: *Circassian Chicken; Pilaff (see page 107); Tomato and Cucumber Salad (see page 106)*
RIGHT: *Gammon with Cumberland Sauce; Vichyssoise (see page 92)*

CHEESE KEBABS

250 g (8 oz)
  chipolata sausages
1 × 227 g (8 oz) can
  pineapple slices
¼ cucumber, cubed
6 tomatoes, quartered
250 g (8 oz)
  Cheddar cheese,
  cubed
12 stoned dates,
  halved
1 grapefruit

Grill the chipolatas, turning frequently, until cooked. Cool and cut into 2.5 cm (1 inch) pieces.

Drain and chop the pineapple. Thread pieces of sausage, pineapple, cucumber, tomato, cheese and date onto cocktail sticks.

Cut a slice from the grapefruit to enable it to stand, cut side down. Stick the small kebabs into the grapefruit.

Makes 24

CHEESE AND NUT CUBES

227 g (8 oz) cottage
  cheese with onion
  and pepper
75 g (3 oz) Double
  Gloucester cheese,
  finely grated
75 g (3 oz) Wensley-
  dale cheese,
  finely grated
3 tablespoons
  asparagus soup
  mix
3 spring onions,
  finely chopped
Tabasco sauce
75 g (3 oz) salted
  peanuts

Place all the cheeses in a bowl. Blend in the soup mix and beat thoroughly. Add the onions and Tabasco to taste.

Shape the mixture into a rectangular block. Wrap in cling film and chill in the refrigerator until firm.

Cut into 2.5 cm (1 inch) cubes. Chop the peanuts very finely, then toss the cheese cubes in them to coat. Arrange on a serving plate and chill until required.

Serves 8 to 10

GARLIC SAUSAGE SPEARS

80 g (2¾ oz)
  Boursin with garlic
75 g (3 oz) medium-
  fat curd cheese
salt
200 g (7 oz) garlic
  sausage, sliced
½ lettuce, shredded

Place the Boursin and curd cheese in a bowl and blend together, adding salt to taste. Divide the mixture between the garlic sausage slices. Roll up and secure each with a cocktail stick.

Arrange the lettuce on a plate and place the spears on top.

Makes about 20

Cheese Kebabs; Cheese and Nut Cubes; Garlic Sausage Spears

SAVOURY STRAWS

125 g (4 oz) plain flour
pinch of salt
pinch of cayenne pepper
50 g (2 oz) margarine
50 g (2 oz) matured Cheddar cheese, grated
1 egg yolk
2 teaspoons tomato ketchup
2-3 teaspoons water
beaten egg to glaze
paprika

Sift the flour, salt and cayenne into a bowl. Rub in the margarine until the mixture resembles breadcrumbs. Stir in the cheese. Add the egg yolk, ketchup and enough water to make a stiff dough.

Turn onto a floured surface and roll out to a rectangle 5 mm (¼ inch) thick. Brush with the egg and sprinkle with paprika. Cut into strips, then cut again to make straws 7.5 cm (3 inches) long. Place on a greased baking sheet and bake in a preheated moderately hot oven, 200°C (400°F), Gas Mark 6, for 10 to 15 minutes until pale golden. Cool on a wire rack.

Arrange the straws on a plate or stand in small pots to serve.

Makes about 50

VARIATION: Cut the pastry into small biscuit rounds with a 4 cm (1½ inch) plain cutter. Cook as above. Top with curd or cream cheese and sprinkle with poppy seeds to serve.

KEEPING FOODS FRESH

Unusual buffet sandwiches or tasty, small canapés can make or ruin your reputation as a party giver if they prove too soggy or dry upon eating.

If you need to make your buffet sandwiches or canapés well ahead of a function and you don't want them to go limp on you, choose bases like crisp toast, fried bread or crispy baked bread. Top with a smear of butter or other waterproof coating to protect the base from moist fillings and toppings. Cover with cling film or foil to prevent drying out.

Alternatively, you can sometimes spoon a thin layer of cool liquid aspic jelly over each canapé or sandwich, which will then set and prevent the topping from drying out.

Do not stack strong-flavoured fillings like tuna and onion next to mild-flavoured cream cheese filling as they will absorb the flavour and smell of the stronger. Finally, store in a cool place like a larder or refrigerator for fresh results.

Open Sandwiches

OPEN SANDWICHES

These are ideal for small buffet parties. Use any of the suggested bases, spread with butter. Place a slice of one of the cheeses on top. Select a topping and one or more of the garnishes to complement the cheese in flavour, but provide contrast in colour. Arrange the open sandwiches on plates.

Bases:
white bread
brown bread
French bread
rye bread
crispbreads

Toppings:
sliced cold meats
salami
pâté
chicken
sardines
prawns

Cheeses:
Cheddar
Leicester
Double Gloucester
Edam
Gouda
Emmental
Gruyère
Jarlsberg
Danish blue vein
Blue Stilton
Cottage cheese
Cream cheese

Garnishes:
onion rings
parsley
cucumber twists
watercress
tomatoes
gherkin fans
olives
hard-boiled eggs
red pepper slices
shredded lettuce
caviar
pineapple
orange slices

ANCHOVY AND PRAWN FONDUE

1 clove garlic, cut
150 ml (¼ pint) dry
    white wine
125 g (4 oz) Gruyère
    cheese, grated
250 g (8 oz) Cheddar
    cheese, grated
1 teaspoon cornflour
2 tablespoons sherry
2 teaspoons anchovy
    essence
Tabasco sauce
cayenne pepper
TO SERVE:
125 g (4 oz) peeled
    prawns
French bread cubes

Rub the inside of a flameproof dish with the cut garlic and pour in the wine. Heat gently until bubbling, then gradually stir in the cheeses. Heat gently, stirring, until the cheese melts and begins to cook.

Blend the cornflour with the sherry and add the anchovy essence, Tabasco and cayenne to taste. Stir into the cheese and heat gently, stirring, for 2 to 3 minutes, until the mixture is thick and creamy.

Serve immediately, with the prawns and bread cubes.
Serves 4 to 6
NOTE: Toasted bread cubes can be served instead of French bread.

AVOCADO AND CHEESE FONDUE

2 avocados
2 tablespoons lemon
    juice
15 g (½ oz) butter
1 clove garlic, crushed
1 onion, finely
    chopped
150 ml (¼ pint) dry
    cider
175 g (6 oz)
    Lancashire cheese,
    crumbled
2 teaspoons cornflour
4 tablespoons single
    cream
salt and pepper
TO SERVE:
French bread cubes
raw vegetables

Peel the avocados, halve and remove the stones. Sprinkle with the lemon juice and mash the avocado flesh, or purée in an electric blender.

Melt the butter in a flameproof dish, add the garlic and onion and fry until soft but not brown. Add the cider and heat until just bubbling, then gradually stir in the cheese. Continue to heat gently until the cheese melts and begins to cook.

Blend the cornflour with the cream and add to the cheese with the avocado purée, and salt and pepper to taste. Heat gently, stirring, for 2 to 3 minutes.

Serve hot, or cold as a dip, with the bread and vegetables, cut into strips.
Serves 4 to 6

LEFT: *Anchovy and Prawn Fondue; Swiss Cheese Fondue; Avocado and Cheese Fondue*
OPPOSITE: *West Country Fondue with other Buffet-fare*

WEST COUNTRY FONDUE

½ small onion, cut
300 ml (½ pint) dry
  cider
1 teaspoon lemon
  juice
500 g (1 lb) Farm-
  house Cheddar
  cheese, grated
1 tablespoon cornflour
2 tablespoons sherry
pinch of dry mustard
1 teaspoon Worcester-
  shire sauce
pepper

Rub the inside of a flameproof dish
with the cut side of the onion. Add
the cider and lemon juice and heat
until bubbling. Gradually stir in the
cheese and heat gently, stirring, until
it melts and begins to cook.

Blend the cornflour with the sherry
and add the mustard, Worcestershire
sauce and pepper to taste. Add to the
cheese and continue to heat, stirring,
for 2 to 3 minutes until the mixture is
thick and creamy. Serve immediately,
with French bread.
Serves 6

SWISS CHEESE FONDUE

1 clove garlic, cut
150 ml (¼ pint) dry
  white wine
1 teaspoon lemon
  juice
175 g (6 oz) Gruyère
  cheese, grated
175 g (6 oz)
  Emmental cheese,
  grated
1 teaspoon cornflour
2 tablespoons kirsch
pepper
grated nutmeg

Rub the inside of a flameproof dish
with the cut garlic. Pour in the wine
and lemon juice and heat gently until
bubbling. Gradually stir in the
cheeses and heat slowly, stirring,
until the cheese melts and begins to
cook.

Blend the cornflour with the
kirsch. Add to the cheese and cook
for 2 to 3 minutes, stirring, until the
mixture is thick and creamy. Add
pepper and nutmeg to taste. Serve
immediately, with French bread.
Serves 4 to 6

PERFECT FONDUES

Cheese fondues can be wonderfully intimate affairs where
numbers are best kept from 4 to 6, or, alternatively, they
may be included as part of a buffet spread.

For best results prepare all food ahead. These tips will
ensure success:
- Warm the wine before adding the cheese and stir
continuously until the cheese is melted.
- Stir fondues in a figure of eight motion – this helps to
blend the cheese into the wine.
- Always keep the flame low, stir frequently and never
allow to boil.
- If a fondue curdles, add a few drops of lemon juice, heat
and stir vigorously.

QUICHE PROVENÇALE

250 g (8 oz) plain
   flour
pinch of salt
75 g (3 oz) butter
25 g (1 oz) lard
1 egg yolk
iced water to mix
FILLING:
25 g (1oz) butter
1 onion, sliced
1 clove garlic, crushed
50 g (2 oz) button
   mushrooms, sliced
1 courgette, chopped
2 large tomatoes,
   skinned and chopped
few basil leaves,
   chopped
½ teaspoon dried
   mixed herbs
salt and pepper
2 eggs
142 ml (5 fl oz)
   single cream
50 g (2 oz) Cheddar
   cheese, grated
25 g (1 oz) Gruyère
   cheese, sliced

Sift the flour and salt into a bowl and rub in the fats until the mixture looks like fine breadcrumbs. Stir in the egg yolk and enough water to make a firm dough. Turn onto a floured surface and knead lightly. Roll out and use to line a 23 cm (9 inch) flan ring placed on a baking sheet. Prick all over and chill for 30 minutes.

Line with foil and dried beans and bake 'blind' in a preheated moderately hot oven, 190°C (375°F), Gas Mark 5, for 12 to 15 minutes, until set. Remove the foil and beans and return to the oven for 5 minutes.

Melt the butter in a pan, add the onion and garlic and cook gently for 5 minutes. Add the vegetables and herbs and season well with salt and pepper. Cook for 10 minutes.

Beat the eggs and cream together and stir in the grated cheese.

Spoon the tomato mixture into the flan case, pour over the egg mixture and carefully arrange the cheese slices on top. Bake for 25 to 30 minutes, until set. Serve hot or cold.
Makes one 23 cm (9 inch) quiche

QUICHE PAYSANNE

75 g (3 oz) plain
   flour, sifted
75 g (3 oz)
   wholemeal flour
pinch of salt
75 g (3 oz) margarine
4-5 tablespoons iced
   water
FILLING:
15 g (½ oz) butter
1 tablespoon oil
4 rashers bacon,
   derinded and
   chopped
1 large onion, chopped
2 potatoes, sliced
2 eggs
142 ml (5 fl oz)
   double cream
1 tablespoon each
   chopped parsley
   and chives
salt and pepper
½ red pepper, cored,
   seeded and chopped
   (optional)
75 g (3 oz) Cheddar
   cheese, grated

Place the flours and salt in a bowl and rub in the margarine until the mixture resembles fine breadcrumbs. Add enough water to make a firm dough. Turn onto a floured surface and knead lightly. Roll out and use to line a 20 cm (8 inch) flan ring on a baking sheet. Prick all over and chill for 30 minutes. Bake blind as for Quiche Provençale (opposite).

Heat the butter and oil in a pan, add the bacon and cook until lightly browned. Drain on kitchen paper. Add the onion and potatoes to the pan and cook for 12 to 15 minutes, until browned. Drain on kitchen paper.

Beat the eggs and cream together, stir in the herbs and season well with salt and pepper.

Spoon the potatoes, onion and bacon into the flan case and sprinkle over the red pepper, if using. Pour over the egg mixture and sprinkle with the cheese. Return to the oven for 20 to 25 minutes, until well risen and golden brown. Serve hot or cold.
Makes one 20 cm (8 inch) quiche

TUNA PRAWN PIZZETTE

1 teaspoon dried yeast
1 teaspoon sugar
350 g (12 oz) strong white plain flour
pinch of salt
125 g (4 oz) butter
2 eggs, beaten
little milk to mix
FILLING:
2 × 64 g (2¼ oz) cans tomato purée
500 g (1 lb) tomatoes, skinned
2 × 99 g (3½ oz) cans tuna, drained
125 g (4 oz) peeled prawns
1 teaspoon each dried oregano and basil
2 tablespoons oil
125 g (4 oz) Bel Paese cheese, cubed
few black olives
2 × 50 g (1¾ oz) cans anchovy fillets

Dissolve the yeast and sugar in a little warm water. Sift the flour and salt into a bowl and rub in the butter until the mixture resembles fine breadcrumbs. Mix in the eggs, dissolved yeast and a little milk to give a firm dough. Knead for about 10 minutes, or until the dough is smooth and elastic. Place in a bowl, cover with a cloth and leave to rise in a warm place for 1½ hours or until doubled in size.

Knead again, divide into 16 pieces and roll out into circles. Place on baking sheets and spread with the tomato purée. Slice the tomatoes and arrange on top. Cover with the tuna and prawns. Sprinkle with herbs and a little oil. Bake in batches in a pre-heated moderately hot oven, 200°C (400°F), Gas Mark 6, for 10 minutes.

Top with the cheese, olives and anchovy fillets. Return to the oven for 5 minutes. Serve hot or cold. **Makes 16 individual pizzas**

Tuna Prawn Pizzette

BACON AND NUT RING

2 tablespoons oil
1 onion, chopped
1 clove garlic, crushed
125 g (4 oz) streaky bacon, derinded and chopped
2 celery sticks, chopped
1 tablespoon wholemeal flour
175 ml (6 fl oz) tomato juice
125 g (4 oz) wholemeal breadcrumbs
125 g (4 oz) hazelnuts, coarsely ground
1 tablespoon rolled oats
1 tablespoon chopped parsley
1 egg, beaten
salt and pepper
watercress to garnish

Heat the oil in a pan, add the onion, garlic, bacon and celery and fry for 4 minutes until softened. Mix in the flour, then add the tomato juice, stirring until the mixture thickens. Add the remaining ingredients, seasoning with ½ teaspoon salt and pepper to taste. Mix thoroughly.

Press the mixture into a greased 19 cm (7½ inch) ring mould and cover with foil. Cook in a preheated moderate oven, 180°C (350°F), Gas Mark 4, for 1 hour.

Turn out onto a serving plate. When cool, garnish with watercress and accompany with a selection of salads.

Serves 4 to 6

NOTE: To cater for a large gathering make 2 or 3 of these rings. For a vegetarian dish, substitute grated cheese for the bacon.

DECORATING THE TABLE

The chances are, unless you are an avid china collector, that you will be limited to one large dinner service and one canteen of cutlery to cope with all of your buffet parties.

The simplest way to ring the changes is to vary your floral table display, napkin colour or shape, table centrepiece, appearance of candles and other decorations.

For a seated table centrepiece it is important to keep the flower height low so that diners have an uninterrupted view but you can go full height when preparing flower decorations for buffet tables.

Follow the seasons for fresh flower arranging – each season offers new scope, new colours and new textures. In Spring opt for new leaves, spring flowers or flowering herbs (they will give fragrance too), during Summer use full-blown flowers or scattered flower petals, in Autumn choose autumn flowers, dried grasses, dried leaves and intersperse with fir cones and acorns, through to Winter where you can mix and match holly and other evergreens with festive decorations like baubles and tinsel.

LEFT: *Quiche Provençale; Quiche Paysanne*

PRAWN CHEESECAKE

125 g (4 oz) butter
250 g (8 oz) Cheddar
  cheese biscuits
4 tablespoons grated
  Parmesan cheese
113 g (4 oz) cream
  cheese
1 teaspoon French
  mustard
125 g (4 oz) Gruyère
  cheese, grated
3 eggs, beaten
142 ml (5 fl oz)
  soured cream
250 g (8 oz) peeled
  prawns, chopped
1 tablespoon each
  chopped parsley
  and chives
4 spring onions,
  chopped
TO GARNISH:
whole cooked prawns
herb sprigs

Melt the butter and crush the biscuits. Combine the butter, biscuit crumbs and 2 tablespoons of the Parmesan cheese. Press onto the base and sides of a 20 cm (8 inch) loose-bottomed flan tin. Chill for 1 hour.

Beat the cream cheese until soft, then stir in the mustard, Gruyère cheese and remaining Parmesan. Gradually stir in the eggs. Fold in the soured cream, prawns, herbs and spring onions.

Spoon the mixture into the prepared flan case and bake in a preheated moderate oven, 180°C (350°F), Gas Mark 4, for 40 to 45 minutes, until golden brown.

Garnish with prawns and sprigs of herbs. Serve cold.
Makes one 20 cm (8 inch) cheesecake

WATERCRESS FLAN

75 g (3 oz) plain
  flour, sifted
75 g (3 oz)
  wholemeal flour
pinch of salt
40 g (1½ oz)
  margarine
40 g (1½ oz) lard
2 tablespoons grated
  Parmesan cheese
1 egg yolk
iced water to mix
FILLING:
25 g (1 oz) butter
1 bunch spring
  onions, chopped
1 bunch watercress,
  finely chopped
3 eggs
142 ml (5 fl oz)
  soured cream
125 g (4 oz) Cheddar
  cheese, grated
TO GARNISH:
watercress sprigs

Place the flours and salt in a bowl and rub in the fats until the mixture resembles fine breadcrumbs. Stir in the Parmesan and egg yolk and add a little water to make a firm dough. Turn onto a floured surface and knead lightly. Roll out and use to line a 20 cm (8 inch) flan ring placed on a baking sheet. Prick all over and chill for 30 minutes. Bake blind as for Quiche Provençale (see page 100).

Melt the butter in a pan, add the onions and cook, without browning, for 5 minutes. Stir in the watercress and cook for 2 minutes, until soft.

Beat the eggs and soured cream together, stir in the cheese and season well with salt and pepper.

Spoon the onion and watercress into the flan case. Pour over the egg mixture and return to the oven for 20 to 25 minutes, until golden brown.

Serve hot or cold, garnished with watercress.
Makes one 20 cm (8 inch) flan

CHEESE AND ONION FLAN

OAT PASTRY:
125 g (4 oz)
  wholemeal flour
125 g (4 oz) medium
  oatmeal
pinch of salt
125 g (4 oz)
  margarine
2-3 tablespoons water
FILLING:
2 tablespoons oil
2 onions, chopped
2 eggs
150 ml (¼ pint) milk
250 g (8 oz)
  Cheddar cheese,
  grated
salt and pepper

Place the flour, oatmeal and salt in a mixing bowl and rub in the margarine until the mixture resembles bread-crumbs. Add the water and mix to a firm dough. Turn onto a floured surface and knead lightly until smooth. Roll out and use to line a 20 cm (8 inch) flan dish. Chill for 15 minutes.

Meanwhile, make the filling. Heat the oil in a pan, add the onions and fry gently until transparent. Mix the eggs and milk together, then stir in the cheese, onions, and salt and pepper to taste.

Pour into the flan case and bake in a preheated moderately hot oven, 190°C (375°F), Gas Mark 5, for 35 to 40 minutes. Serve hot or cold.
Makes one 20 cm (8 inch) flan

SAVOURY CHEESE HORNS

1 × 368 g (13 oz)
    packet frozen puff
    pastry, thawed
beaten egg to glaze
FILLING:
142 ml (5 fl oz)
    double cream,
    whipped
125 g (4 oz) red
    Cheshire cheese,
    finely grated
50 g (2 oz) blue
    Cheshire cheese,
    finely grated
pinch of cayenne
    pepper
pinch of dry mustard
1 tablespoon chopped
    parsley
salt and pepper

Roll out the pastry into a rectangle, about 25 × 30 cm (10 × 12 inches), and trim the edges. Cut into 12 strips, about 2.5 cm (1 inch) wide. Dampen one long edge of each strip and wind around 12 greased horn cases, starting at the pointed end, and overlapping by about 5 mm (¼ inch). Gently press the edges together.

Place on a dampened baking sheet and brush with beaten egg. Bake in a preheated hot oven, 230°C (450°F), Gas Mark 8, for 10 to 15 minutes. Remove from the cases and return to the oven for 5 minutes. Cool on a wire rack.

Combine the cream, cheeses, cayenne, mustard, parsley, and salt and pepper to taste. Spoon the filling into the cases just before serving.
Makes 12

Courgette Flan

COURGETTE FLAN

175 g (6 oz) plain
    flour
pinch of salt
75 g (3 oz) butter or
    margarine
2 tablespoons cold
    water
    (approximately)
FILLING:
500 g (1 lb)
    courgettes
125 g (4 oz)
    Cheddar cheese
284 ml (10 fl oz)
    single cream
3 eggs, beaten
salt and pepper

Sift flour and salt into a bowl and rub in the fat until the mixture resembles fine breadcrumbs. Add enough water to mix to a firm dough. Turn onto a floured surface and knead lightly.

Roll out the pastry and use to line a 25 cm (10 inch) flan tin. Bake blind in a preheated moderately hot oven, 200°C (400°F), Gas Mark 6, for 10 minutes. Remove from the oven and lower the temperature to 160°C (325°F), Gas Mark 3.

Arrange the courgettes in the flan case. Finely grate the cheese into a bowl. Gradually beat the cream, eggs, and salt and pepper to taste, into the cheese until combined. Pour over the courgettes. Return to the oven and bake for 30 to 40 minutes, until set. Serve hot or cold.
Makes one 25 cm (10 inch) flan

CHEESE AND APRICOT WHIRLS

113 g (4 oz) cream
    cheese
3 tablespoons milk
50 g (2 oz) matured
    Cheddar cheese,
    finely grated
salt and pepper
1 × 411 g (14½ oz)
    can apricot halves,
    drained thoroughly
TO GARNISH:
paprika
walnut pieces
shredded lettuce

Place the cream cheese in a bowl and beat with a wooden spoon to soften. Blend in the milk and Cheddar, then add salt and pepper to taste.

Place the mixture in a piping bag fitted with a 1 cm (½ inch) star nozzle and pipe a whirl of filling into each apricot half. Sprinkle with paprika and top with walnut pieces.

Arrange the lettuce on a serving plate and place the apricots on top.
Makes about 10
NOTE: Any remaining cheese mixture can be piped onto savoury biscuits.

OPPOSITE: *Prawn Cheesecake*

Pepper and Salami Salad

PEPPER AND SALAMI SALAD

4 each large green,
   red and yellow
   peppers
12 tomatoes
8 hard-boiled eggs
125 g (4 oz) each
   garlic sausage and
   French salami
4 × 50 g (1¾ oz)
   cans anchovy
   fillets, drained
black olives
DRESSING:
4 cloves garlic, crushed
2 tablespoons each
   chopped parsley,
   chives, tarragon
   and chervil
2 teaspoons Meaux
   mustard
2 teaspoons clear honey
6 tablespoons lemon
   juice
12 tablespoons olive oil
salt and pepper

Place the whole peppers under a preheated hot grill until the skins are charred. Leave to cool, then peel away the skin, remove the cores and seeds, and slice the flesh.

Thickly slice the tomatoes and eggs and divide between 2 salad bowls. Chop the garlic sausage and salami and sprinkle into the bowls. Place the peppers around the edge.

Arrange the anchovy fillets in a lattice over the salads and place the olives on top.

Mix the dressing ingredients together in a bowl, seasoning with salt and pepper to taste. Spoon half over each salad.

Chill for 20 minutes before serving.
Serves 20

CRISPY LETTUCE AND CAULIFLOWER SALAD

2 red-skinned dessert
   apples
2 tablespoons lemon
   juice
1 large Iceberg lettuce
1 large cauliflower
6 slices garlic sausage,
   cut into strips
300 ml (½ pint)
   mayonnaise
142 ml (5 fl oz)
   soured cream
1 tablespoon curry
   powder

Cut the apples into quarters, remove the cores, then slice the apples thinly. Sprinkle the lemon juice over the apple slices to prevent browning. Place in a large salad bowl.

Shred the lettuce and break the cauliflower into florets. Add to the apple slices with the garlic sausage.

Blend the mayonnaise, soured cream and curry powder together in a small bowl. Pour over the salad just before serving, tossing well.
Serves 20

POTATO SALAD

1.5 kg (3 lb) new
   potatoes
salt
1 bunch spring
   onions, sliced
2 celery sticks, finely
   sliced
1 × 500 g (1.1 lb)
   jar mayonnaise
1 tablespoon chopped
   parsley

Cook the potatoes in their skins in boiling salted water until cooked but still firm. Drain and carefully peel off skins, then dice. Place in a salad bowl with the spring onions and celery; add the mayonnaise and toss until the potatoes are well coated. Sprinkle with parsley to serve.
Serves 20

RADICCHIO SALAD

1 head of curly endive
2 heads of radicchio
2 large heads of
   chicory
8 tablespoons Lime
   vinaigrette dressing
   (see page 153)
50 g (2 oz) pine nuts

Separate the endive and radicchio into leaves, tear into pieces and place in a bowl. Cut the chicory diagonally across into 1 cm (½ inch) slices and add to the bowl. Pour over the dressing and toss well.

Transfer to a salad bowl and sprinkle with the pine nuts to serve.
Serves 12

OPPOSITE: *Avocado Salad; Chicory and Orange Salad; Watercress and Tofu Salad; Radicchio Salad*

AVOCADO SALAD

1 head of curly endive
2 bunches of
   watercress
4 avocado pears,
   halved and stoned
12 tablespoons
   French dressing
   (see page 151)

Tear the endive into pieces and separate the watercress into sprigs; place in a large salad bowl.

Peel the avocados and slice into a bowl. Pour over the dressing and toss until coated. Add to the endive and watercress and toss thoroughly.
Serves 12

WATERCRESS AND TOFU SALAD

2 × 300 g (10 oz)
   cake of tofu
4 tablespoons sesame
   seeds, roasted
8 tablespoons Soy
   sauce dressing (see
   page 153)
4 bunches of
   watercress

Cut the tofu into 1 cm (½ inch) cubes. Place in a bowl with the sesame seeds, pour over the dressing and toss carefully. Divide watercress into sprigs, add to the tofu and mix gently. Transfer to a large salad bowl.
Serves 10 to 12
NOTE: Tofu is a soya bean curd with a soft delicate texture, sold in slabs.

CHICORY AND ORANGE SALAD

6 heads of chicory
6 oranges
2 tablespoons
   chopped parsley
8 tablespoons Honey
   and lemon dressing
   (see page 151)

Cut the chicory diagonally across into 1 cm (½ inch) slices and place in a large salad bowl. Remove the peel and pith from the oranges and break into segments, holding the fruit over the bowl so that any juice is included.

Add the parsley and dressing and toss thoroughly just before serving.
Serves 10 to 12

SALAD DRESSINGS

A well made salad dressing can transform a good salad into something really exciting. But it is most important to use good ingredients; the choice of oil is especially important. Oils are produced from various nuts, seeds and beans, and each has its own particular flavour. Unrefined oils have a superior flavour, especially olive oil, and are more expensive than refined oils. Always choose wine, cider or herb-flavoured vinegars – malt vinegar is far too harsh. Refer to pages 151 to 153 for delicious dressing recipes.

CHICK PEA SALAD

500 g (1 lb) chick
 peas
2 onions, finely
 chopped
4 cloves garlic, crushed
2 red peppers, cored,
 seeded and sliced
2 green peppers, cored,
 seeded and sliced
4 tablespoons chopped
 mixed herbs (e.g.
 parsley, chives,
 fennel, marjoram)
350 g (12 oz)
 Danish Havarti
 cheese, cubed
DRESSING:
1 teaspoon mustard
1 teaspoon sugar
2 tablespoons wine
 vinegar
8 tablespoons oil
salt and pepper
TO GARNISH:
chopped parsley

Soak the chick peas in cold water overnight, drain and place in a saucepan. Cover with cold water and bring to the boil. Boil for 10 minutes, then lower the heat, cover and simmer for 1 hour or until soft. Drain and rinse with cold water.

Place in a bowl with the onion, garlic, peppers, herbs and cheese.

To make the dressing, blend the mustard and sugar with the vinegar, then beat in the oil. Add salt and pepper to taste. Pour the dressing over the salad. Mix thoroughly and turn into a serving bowl. Sprinkle with parsley to serve.

Serves 12

TOMATO AND CUCUMBER SALAD

2 cucumbers
2 kg (4½ lb) tomatoes
250 g (8 oz) Lanca-
 shire cheese, grated
4 tablespoons chopped
 chives or parsley
DRESSING:
150 ml (¼ pint)
 olive oil
4 tablespoons white
 wine vinegar
1 teaspoon sugar
1 teaspoon dry mustard
2 cloves garlic, crushed
salt and pepper

Thinly slice the cucumbers and tomatoes into a large salad bowl. Sprinkle with the cheese and herbs.

Put all the dressing ingredients, with salt and pepper to taste, in a screw-top jar and shake well. Pour over the salad just before serving, tossing lightly.

Serves 30
(Illustrated on page 94)

BROAD BEAN AND CARROT SALAD

1 kg (2 lb) frozen
 broad beans
250 g (8 oz) carrots,
 grated
150 ml (¼ pint)
 French dressing
 (see page 151)
1 tablespoon chopped
 chives

Put the frozen broad beans in a bowl and pour over boiling water to cover; leave for 2 minutes, then drain and pop off the skins. Mix with the carrots in a serving bowl. Pour over the French dressing and toss lightly.

Sprinkle with chopped chives to serve.

Serves 20

SALADS FOR BUFFETS

Salads should always be left to the very last minute in terms of preparation even for a buffet party spread. If you are still concerned that upon standing they will lose some of their crisp texture then why not add a few crunchy croûtons for flavour and bite?

To make croûtons, fry cubes of one-day old bread in hot oil for 1-2 minutes until golden and crisp then drain on absorbent kitchen towels. Toss in a little grated Parmesan cheese, crushed sea salt or chopped herbs if liked. Sprinkle over a salad to serve.

LEFT: Chick Pea Salad
OPPOSITE: Wensleydale Fruit Salad

SAFFRON SALAD

4 cloves garlic
2 teaspoons French
    mustard
2 teaspoons clear honey
150 ml (¼ pint) olive
    oil
4 tablespoons lemon
    or lime juice
salt and pepper
2 tablespoons each
    chopped parsley
    and chives
250 g (8 oz) raisins
4 onions, chopped
500 g (1 lb) long-
    grain rice
pinch of saffron strands
600 ml (1 pint) stock
125 g (4 oz) each
    salted peanuts and
    cashew nuts
250 g (8 oz) streaky
    bacon, derinded
lemon or lime slices to
    garnish

Slice 2 garlic cloves and set aside; crush the remaining cloves and place in a salad bowl with the mustard and honey. Stir in 8 tablespoons of the oil and the lemon or lime juice. Season well with salt and pepper. Stir in the parsley, chives and raisins.

Heat the remaining oil in a pan, add the sliced garlic and the onions and fry until browned. Stir in the rice, saffron and stock. Season with salt to taste, bring to the boil and cook for 12 minutes. Drain and leave to cool, then stir into the oil and lemon juice mixture with the nuts.

Cook the bacon under a preheated hot grill until crisp. Crumble and sprinkle over the rice. Garnish with lemon or lime slices.
Serves 15
NOTE: Use well-flavoured vegetable or chicken stock.

WENSLEYDALE FRUIT SALAD

PILAFF

150 ml (¼ pint)
    sunflower oil
1 kg (2 lb) long-
    grain rice
1 litre (1¾ pints)
    water
4 teaspoons salt
500 g (1 lb) onions,
    chopped
6 fat cloves garlic,
    sliced
125 g (4 oz)
    blanched whole
    almonds
125 g (4 oz) raisins
500 g (1 lb)
    tomatoes, skinned,
    seeded and chopped

Heat 5 tablespoons of the oil in a large pan and add the rice, water and salt. Bring to the boil, cover tightly and simmer for about 15 minutes, until the liquid is absorbed and the rice is tender.

Meanwhile, heat the remaining oil in another pan, add the onions, garlic and almonds and fry until golden. Add the raisins and tomatoes and cook for 5 minutes.

Transfer the rice to a large warmed serving dish, flaking with a fork to separate the grains. Pour the onion and tomato mixture from the pan over the rice and mix in with a fork until well blended. Serve hot.
Serves 30
(Illustrated on page 94)

4 red dessert apples
lemon juice
1 honeydew melon
2 × 227 g (8 oz) cans
    pineapple slices
125 g (4 oz) dates,
    stoned and chopped
4 tablespoons diced
    cucumber
4 celery sticks,
    chopped
350 g (12 oz)
    Wensleydale
    cheese, cubed
300 g (10 oz) natural
    yogurt
2 teaspoons sugar
    (optional)
lettuce to serve

Core and slice the apples and toss in lemon juice to prevent discoloration. Remove the skin from the melon and discard the seeds. Scoop the flesh into balls, using a melon baller, or cut into dice. Drain the pineapple and cut into bite-size pieces.

Mix together the apple, melon, pineapple, dates, cucumber, celery and cheese in a bowl. Stir in the yogurt and sugar, if using. Toss together well.

Pile the salad into a serving bowl lined with lettuce leaves. Serve immediately.
Serves 12

Chocolate Brandy Gâteau

CHOCOLATE BRANDY GÂTEAU

350 g (12 oz) plain
 chocolate, broken
 into pieces
4 tablespoons strong
 black coffee
4 tablespoons brandy
250 g (8 oz)
 digestive biscuits,
 broken into small
 pieces
175 g (6 oz) glacé
 cherries, quartered
TO FINISH:
250 ml (8 fl oz)
 double cream,
 whipped
chocolate caraque,
 made with 50 g
 (2 oz) chocolate
 (see below)

Place the chocolate and coffee in a pan and heat gently until melted; do not allow to become more than lukewarm. Remove from the heat and add the brandy, biscuits and cherries. Mix thoroughly, then turn into a greased 18 cm (7 inch) loose-bottomed cake tin. Smooth the top and chill overnight in the refrigerator.

Remove from the tin and slide onto a plate. Pipe the cream over the top of the gâteau. Decorate with chocolate caraque.

Serves 8

Chocolate Caraque: Spread a thin layer of melted chocolate onto a marble slab. Leave until firm, but not hard. Draw a sharp, thin-bladed knife at a slight angle across the chocolate with a slight sawing movement, scraping off thin layers to form long scrolls.

ORANGE HALVA CAKE

CAKE MIXTURE:
175 g (6 oz) butter
175 g (6 oz) caster
 sugar
grated rind and juice
 of 1 orange
3 eggs, beaten
275 g (9 oz) semolina
125 g (4 oz) ground
 almonds
3 teaspoons baking
 powder
SYRUP:
175 g (6 oz) caster
 sugar
5 tablespoons water
2 tablespoons lemon
 juice
1/2 teaspoon ground
 cinnamon
25 g (1 oz) chopped
 candied peel
3 tablespoons orange
 juice
TO DECORATE:
142 ml (5 fl oz)
 whipping cream,
 whipped
25 g (1 oz) flaked
 almonds, toasted

Cream the butter and sugar together with the grated orange rind until pale and fluffy. Beat in the orange juice and eggs, then fold in the semolina, ground almonds and baking powder.

Turn into a greased and floured 23 cm (9 inch) ring mould. Bake in a preheated hot oven, 220°C (425°F), Gas Mark 7, for 10 minutes, then lower the heat to 180°C (350°F), Gas Mark 4, and bake for a further 30 minutes.

Meanwhile prepare the syrup. Place the sugar, water, lemon juice, cinnamon and peel in a pan and bring to the boil, stirring. Simmer until slightly thickened, then add the orange juice.

Turn the cake onto a serving plate straight from the oven. Pour the syrup over the hot cake slowly until it is all absorbed. Leave to cool.

To serve, fill the centre of the ring with the whipped cream and sprinkle the almonds on the cake.

Serves 10

SAVING THE DAY

The worst that can happen with any entertaining event is a culinary disaster. However, unless the food you have cooked is charred beyond recognition there are a few tips that can save the day!

Always follow the cooking times in the recipes carefully but should you over-cook vegetables then purée them with a little cream as a delicious alternative. If a soup or casserole is accidentally over-seasoned then stir in a little flavour-stretching yogurt. Or, if a pudding fails to come out of its mould intact then pile into a pretty bowl and decorate it imaginatively – call it a house 'surprise' and serve with panache!

Chocolate Chestnut Charlotte; Chocolate Orange Cheesecake

CHOCOLATE CHESTNUT CHARLOTTE

125 g (4 oz) plain chocolate, chopped
300 ml (½ pint) milk
2 eggs, separated
50 g (2 oz) soft light brown sugar
15 g (½ oz) gelatine, soaked in 3 tablespoons cold water
½ × 439 g (15½ oz) can unsweetened chestnut purée
284 ml (10 fl oz) double cream, whipped
30 Langue de Chat biscuits
chocolate triangles (see below)

Gently heat the chocolate in a small pan with the milk until melted.

Beat the egg yolks and sugar until creamy, then stir in the chocolate. Return to pan and heat gently, stirring until thickened. Stir in the gelatine.

Beat the chestnut purée with a little of the custard until smooth, then mix in the remainder. Cool, then fold in two thirds of the cream. Whisk the egg whites until stiff and fold in. Turn into a lightly oiled deep 18 cm (7 inch) cake tin and chill until set.

Turn out onto a plate and cover with a thin layer of cream. Press the biscuits around the side; trim to fit if necessary. Decorate with remaining cream and chocolate triangles.
Serves 8
Chocolate Triangles: Thinly spread melted chocolate on greaseproof paper. When just set, cut into triangles.

CHOCOLATE ORANGE CHEESECAKE

50 g (2 oz) butter
125 g (4 oz) digestive biscuits, finely crushed
25 g (1 oz) demerara sugar
454 g (1 lb) curd cheese
50 g (2 oz) caster sugar
grated rind and juice of 2 oranges
250 ml (8 fl oz) single cream
15 g (½ oz) gelatine, soaked in 3 tablespoons cold water
50 g (2 oz) plain chocolate, melted
whipped cream to decorate

Melt the butter in a pan and stir in the biscuit crumbs and sugar. Spread the mixture over the base of a greased 20 cm (8 inch) loose-bottomed cake tin and press down. Leave in the refrigerator until firm.

Place the cheese in a bowl with the sugar and orange rind and beat until smooth. Strain the orange juice and add to the mixture, then gradually stir in the cream.

Heat the gelatine gently until dissolved, then stir into the cheese mixture. Pour over the crumb base. Pour the cooled, melted chocolate over the top, swirling with a fork to give a marbled effect. Chill in the refrigerator until set.

Remove from the tin and place on a serving plate. Pipe cream around the edge to serve.
Serves 8

CHOCOLATE AND ORANGE MOUSSE

250 g (8 oz) plain
  chocolate, broken
  into pieces
5 tablespoons water
4 eggs
2 egg yolks
75 g (3 oz) caster
  sugar
grated rind and juice
  of 1 orange
15 g (½ oz) gelatine
284 ml (10 fl oz)
  whipping cream,
  whipped
50 g (2 oz) plain
  chocolate, grated,
  to decorate

Place the chocolate and water in a small pan and heat gently until melted, then cool.

Whisk the eggs, egg yolks, sugar and orange rind in a bowl over a pan of boiling water, until thick and mousse-like.

Soak the gelatine in the orange juice, adding water to make up to 3 tablespoons if necessary. Place in a bowl over a pan of simmering water and stir until dissolved, then add to the mousse with the chocolate. Stir over a bowl of iced water until thickening, then fold in half the cream and turn into a serving bowl.

Decorate with the remaining cream and the grated chocolate.
Serves 6 to 8

CHESTNUT ROULADE

3 eggs, separated
125 g (4 oz) caster
  sugar
½ × 439 g
  (15½ oz) can
  unsweetened
  chestnut purée
grated rind and juice
  of 1 orange
sifted icing sugar for
  sprinkling
284 ml (10 fl oz)
  double cream
2 tablespoons Grand
  Marnier
finely shredded
  orange rind to
  decorate

Whisk the egg yolks with the sugar until thick and creamy. Put the chestnut purée in a bowl with the orange juice and beat until blended, then whisk into the egg mixture. Whisk the egg whites until fairly stiff and fold in carefully.

Turn into a lined and greased 20 × 30 cm (8 × 12 inch) Swiss roll tin. Bake in a preheated moderate oven, 180°C (350°F), Gas Mark 4, for 25 to 30 minutes, until firm.

Cool for 5 minutes, then cover with a clean damp cloth and leave until cold. Carefully turn the roulade onto a sheet of greaseproof paper, sprinkled thickly with icing sugar. Peel off the lining paper.

Place the cream, orange rind and liqueur in a bowl and whip until stiff. Spread three-quarters over the roulade and roll up like a Swiss roll. Transfer to a serving dish, pipe the remaining cream along the top and decorate with orange rind.
Serves 8

CHOCOLATE AND ORANGE ICE CREAM

2 egg yolks
50 g (2 oz) caster
  sugar
grated rind and juice
  of 1 orange
175 g (6 oz) plain
  chocolate, chopped
284 ml (10 fl oz)
  single cream
284 ml (10 fl oz)
  double cream,
  whipped
finely shredded
  orange rind, to
  decorate

Beat the egg yolks, sugar and orange rind together. Put the chocolate and single cream in a heatproof bowl over a pan of simmering water until melted. Pour onto the egg mixture, stirring vigorously, then return to the bowl and heat gently until thickened. Add the orange juice; leave to cool.

Fold in three quarters of the double cream and turn into a 900 ml (1½ pint) loaf tin. Cover with foil, seal and freeze until firm.

Turn out onto a plate 30 minutes before serving. Decorate with the remaining cream and orange rind and allow to soften in the refrigerator.
Serves 6

LEFT: *Chestnut Roulade*
OPPOSITE: *Irish Coffee Soufflé; Hazelnut Meringues with Caramel Sauce*

IRISH COFFEE SOUFFLÉ

*15 g (½ oz)
   powdered gelatine*
*250 ml (8 fl oz)
   strong black coffee*
6 eggs, separated
175 g (6 oz) sugar
*150 ml (¼ pint)
   Irish whiskey*
*284 ml (10 fl oz)
   double cream*
*125 g (4 oz)
   walnuts, finely
   chopped*
*whipped cream and
   walnut halves to
   decorate*

Lightly grease a 1 litre (2 pint) soufflé dish and tie a band of greaseproof paper around the outside of the dish to extend 5 cm (2 inches) above the rim. Grease the inside of the paper collar.

Dissolve the gelatine in the coffee. Cool slightly. Whisk the egg yolks with the sugar in a basin over a pan of hot water until the mixture is very thick and light. (If using an electric beater, no heat is needed.)

Remove from the heat and gradually whisk in the whiskey and the coffee mixture. Place the bowl in another bowl containing ice cubes and chill, whisking occasionally, until the mixture is the consistency of unbeaten egg white.

Whisk the egg whites until stiff. Whip the cream until thick. Fold the cream into the coffee mixture, followed by the egg whites. Spoon into the prepared soufflé dish. Chill for at least 3 hours or until set.

To serve, remove the paper collar and press the chopped walnuts onto the side. Decorate the top with whirls of cream and walnut halves.

Serves 6 to 8

HAZELNUT MERINGUES WITH CARAMEL SAUCE

4 egg whites
*250 g (8 oz) caster
   sugar*
*50 g (2 oz) toasted
   hazelnuts, very
   finely chopped*
*vanilla or chocolate
   ice cream to serve*
SAUCE:
*250 g (8 oz)
   caramels, chopped*
*284 ml (10 fl oz)
   double cream*

Whisk the egg whites until stiff. Add 4 teaspoons of the sugar and continue whisking for 1 minute. Fold in the remaining sugar and the hazelnuts. Spoon or pipe 12 hazelnut meringue shells on baking sheets lined with non-stick paper. Sprinkle with a little extra caster sugar.

Place in a preheated very cool oven, 120°C (250°F), Gas Mark ½, for 1 hour, changing the baking sheets around halfway through the cooking.

Carefully lift the meringues from the baking sheets and press in the soft undersides. Replace on the sheets, undersides up, and return to the oven for a further 20 minutes or until completely dry. Cool.

To make the sauce, put the caramel pieces and cream into a saucepan and heat gently, stirring, until melted. If the sauce is too thick, add a little milk.

To serve, sandwich together pairs of meringue shells with ice cream and spoon over the sauce.

Serves 6

HAZELNUT MERINGUE LAYER

MERINGUE:
4 egg whites
250 g (8 oz) caster
  sugar
125 g (4 oz)
  hazelnuts, roasted
  and ground
FILLING:
284 ml (10 fl oz)
  double cream
125 g (4 oz)
  hazelnut chocolate
  spread
TO DECORATE:
25 g (1 oz) plain
  chocolate, melted
10 roasted hazelnuts

Place the egg whites in a bowl and whisk until stiff, then gradually whisk in half of the sugar. Carefully fold in the remaining sugar and the ground nuts.

Spread the meringue into two 23 cm (9 inch) circles on a baking sheet lined with silicone paper.

Bake them in a preheated cool oven, 140°C (275°F), Gas Mark 1, for 2½ hours until crisp. Carefully remove from the paper; cool on a wire rack.

Whip the cream and hazelnut spread together until it forms soft peaks. Using one-third of the cream, sandwich the meringues together. Spread another third of the cream on top.

Drizzle the chocolate on top of the gâteau. Pipe on the remaining cream and top with the hazelnuts.
Serves 8 to 10

PARIS BREST WITH GINGER

CHOUX PASTRY:
300 ml (½ pint)
  water
125 g (4 oz) butter
150 g (5 oz) plain
  flour, sifted
½ teaspoon vanilla
  essence
4 eggs, beaten
50 g (2 oz) flaked
  almonds
FILLING:
125 g (4 oz)
  preserved ginger,
  chopped
284 ml (10 fl oz)
  whipping cream,
  whipped with
  1 tablespoon syrup
  from the ginger
TO FINISH:
50 g (2 oz) icing
  sugar

Heat the water and butter in a pan slowly until the butter melts. Bring to the boil, add the flour all at once and beat until the mixture leaves the side of the pan. Cool slightly, then add the essence. Reserve one spoonful of egg, then gradually add remainder to the pan, beating well after each addition.

Spoon the choux pastry into a 25 cm (10 inch) ring on a greased baking sheet. Brush with the reserved egg and sprinkle with the almonds. Bake in a preheated hot oven, 220°C (425°F), Gas Mark 7, for 15 minutes. Lower the heat to 190°C (375°F), Gas Mark 5 and bake for a further 25 minutes, until golden.

Split the cake horizontally. Scoop out any uncooked pastry and return the halves to the oven for 5 minutes.

Fold the ginger into the whipped cream and use to sandwich the cake together. Sprinkle with icing sugar.
Serves 8 to 10

STRAWBERRY SHORTCAKE

125 g (4 oz) butter
50 g (2 oz) caster sugar
125 g (4 oz) plain flour, sifted
50 g (2 oz) cornflour, sifted
250 g (8 oz) strawberries
284 ml (10 fl oz) double cream, whipped
sifted icing sugar for dredging

Cream the butter and sugar together until soft and creamy, then stir in the flour and cornflour. Mix to a firm dough, then turn onto a floured surface and knead lightly. Divide the mixture in half. Roll each piece into a 20 cm (8 inch) round on a baking sheet.

Bake in a preheated moderate oven, 180°C (350°F), Gas Mark 4, for 20 minutes. Leave for a few minutes, then mark one round into 6 sections. Carefully slide both rounds onto a wire rack to cool.

Slice the strawberries lengthwise. Set aside 6 slices for decoration. Mix three-quarters of the cream with the strawberries and spread over the plain round of shortcake. Break the other round into sections and place on top. Sprinkle with icing sugar. Pipe a cream rosette on each section and decorate with the reserved strawberry slices.

Serves 6

CHOCOLATE CUPS

284 ml (10 fl oz) single cream
250 g (8 oz) plain chocolate, chopped
4 egg yolks
3 tablespoons brandy
chocolate curls to decorate (see below)

Place the cream in a pan and heat just to boiling point. Pour into a blender or food processor and add the chocolate. Blend on maximum speed for 30 seconds. Add the egg yolks and brandy and blend for 10 seconds. Pour into glasses or small cups and chill until required. Sprinkle with chocolate curls to serve.

Serves 8

Chocolate Curls: Shave thin layers from a block of chocolate with a potato peeler.

OPPOSITE: *Hazelnut Meringue Layer; Paris Brest with Ginger*
RIGHT: *Melon Jelly Salad*

MELON JELLY SALAD

1 large Ogen melon, halved and seeded
250 g (8 oz) black grapes, halved and seeded
2 kiwi fruit, peeled and thinly sliced
150 ml (¼ pint) water
50 g (2 oz) caster sugar
thinly pared rind and juice of 1 lemon
25 g (1 oz) gelatine, soaked in 6 tablespoons cold water
150 ml (¼ pint) white wine
142 ml (5 fl oz) double cream, whipped

Scoop the flesh from the melon halves with a melon baller, or cut into cubes, and place in a bowl with the grapes and kiwi fruit.

Put the water, sugar and lemon rind in a pan and heat gently to dissolve the sugar. Simmer for 5 minutes, then add the soaked gelatine and stir until dissolved. Leave to cool, then add the lemon juice and wine. Strain into the bowl of fruit.

Pour into individual glasses and chill until set. Decorate with the whipped cream to serve, or serve the cream separately.

Serves 4

RASPBERRY GÂTEAU

3 eggs, separated
125 g (4 oz) caster
   sugar
grated rind and juice
   of ½ lemon
50 g (2 oz) semolina
25 g (1 oz) ground
   almonds
TO FINISH:
284 ml (10 fl oz)
   double cream,
   whipped
250 g (8 oz)
   raspberries
4 tablespoons
   redcurrant jelly
2 teaspoons water
50 g (2 oz) blanched
   almonds, chopped
   and toasted

Whisk the egg yolks with the sugar, lemon rind and juice until thick and creamy. Stir in the semolina and ground almonds. Whisk the egg whites until stiff and fold into the mixture.

Turn into a lined, greased and floured 20 cm (8 inch) cake tin. Bake in a preheated moderate oven, 180°C (350°F), Gas Mark 4, for 35 to 40 minutes. Turn onto a wire rack to cool.

Split the cake in half. Sandwich together with three-quarters of the cream. Arrange the raspberries on the top, leaving a border around the edge.

Heat the redcurrant jelly with the water. Use this glaze to brush the raspberries and the sides of the cake. Coat the sides with the almonds. Pipe the remaining cream around the top.
Serves 6

STRAWBERRY CHOUX RING

CHOUX PASTRY:
50 g (2 oz) butter or
   margarine
150 ml (¼ pint)
   water
65 g (2½ oz) plain
   flour, sifted
2 eggs, beaten
25 g (1 oz) flaked
   almonds
FILLING:
284 ml (10 fl oz)
   double cream
1 tablespoon caster
   sugar
350 g (12 oz)
   strawberries,
   halved
TO FINISH:
sifted icing sugar

Make the choux pastry as for Profiteroles (see right). Spoon onto a dampened baking sheet to form a 20 cm (8 inch) ring. Sprinkle with the almonds and bake in a preheated hot oven, 220°C (425°F), Gas Mark 7, for 15 minutes. Lower the heat to 190°C (375°F), Gas Mark 5, and bake for a further 20 to 25 minutes until golden brown. Cool on a wire rack.

Whip the cream until it holds its shape, then fold in the caster sugar and 250 g (8 oz) of the strawberries.

Split the ring in half horizontally and pile the filling into the hollow bottom half. Cover with the remaining strawberries then replace the top half of the choux ring. Sprinkle with icing sugar.
Serves 6

PROFITEROLES

CHOUX PASTRY:
50 g (2 oz) butter or
   margarine
150 ml (¼ pint)
   water
65 g (2½ oz) plain
   flour, sifted
2 eggs, beaten
CHOCOLATE SAUCE:
175 g (6 oz) plain
   chocolate
150 ml (¼ pint)
   water
1 teaspoon instant
   coffee powder
125 g (4 oz) sugar
FILLING:
1 tablespoon icing
   sugar, sifted
2-3 drops vanilla
   essence
170 ml (6 fl oz)
   double cream,
   whipped

Melt the fat in a large pan, add the water and bring to the boil. Add the flour all at once and beat until the mixture leaves the sides of the pan. Cool slightly, then add the eggs a little at a time, beating vigorously.

Put the mixture into a piping bag, fitted with a plain 1 cm (½ inch) nozzle, and pipe small mounds on a dampened baking sheet.

Bake in a preheated hot oven, 220°C (425°F), Gas Mark 7, for 10 minutes, then lower the heat to 190°C (375°F), Gas Mark 5, and bake for a further 20 to 25 minutes until golden. Make a slit in the side of each bun. Cool on a wire rack.

To make the sauce: gently melt together the chocolate, 2 tablespoons of the water and the coffee in a small pan. Add the remaining water and the sugar and heat gently, stirring, until dissolved, then simmer, uncovered, for 10 minutes. Leave to cool.

To make the filling: fold the sugar and essence into the cream. Pipe or spoon a little into each profiterole.

Pile the profiteroles on a serving dish. Pour over the chocolate sauce.
Serves 4 to 6

CENTREPIECE DISPLAYS

If you are holding a celebratory buffet party then you will probably have a cake as a special party centrepiece – be it birthday, christening, anniversary or engagement.

If you have nothing so specific to celebrate then why not consider a frosted fruit centrepiece as the focal point for the buffet table spread – on the culinary front nothing looks more spectacular.

To frost, dip fruits like apples, plums, grapes and pears into lightly-beaten egg white and then into caster sugar and leave until dry. When very dry arrange attractively in a fruit bowl or on a cake stand. Add other seasonal decorations like grasses, baubles, fresh herbs, ribbons or flowers for a beautiful effect.

Raspberry Gâteau; Strawberry Choux Ring; Profiteroles

CHOCOLATE AND APRICOT GÂTEAU

300 g (10 oz) plain flour
50 g (2 oz) cocoa powder
1/2 teaspoon salt
4 teaspoons baking powder
300 g (10 oz) soft brown sugar
4 eggs, separated
175 ml (6 fl oz) corn oil
175 ml (6 fl oz) milk
1 teaspoon vanilla essence

FILLING AND TOPPING:
1 × 411 g (14 1/2 oz) can apricot halves
2 tablespoons rum or apricot liqueur
1/2 × 340 g (12 oz) jar apricot conserve
284 ml (10 fl oz) whipping cream, whipped
25 g (1 oz) plain chocolate

Sift the flour, cocoa, salt and baking powder into a bowl. Stir in the sugar, then add the egg yolks, oil, milk and vanilla essence. Beat well until smooth. Whisk the egg whites and fold into the mixture.

Pour into a lined and greased 25 cm (10 inch) deep cake tin and bake in a preheated moderate oven, 180°C (350°F), Gas Mark 4, for 50 minutes to 1 hour until risen and firm to the touch. Leave in the tin.

Drain the juice from the apricots into a small pan. Add the rum or liqueur and heat gently. Pour all over the top of the cake and leave in the tin until cold, then remove.

Split the cake in half and sandwich together with the apricot conserve. Place the cake on a serving plate and cover completely with the cream, spreading it on with a palette knife.

Arrange the apricots cut side down around the top edge of the cake.

Using a potato peeler, peel the chocolate to make curls. Sprinkle over the top of the cake to complete the decoration.
Serves 10

SUMMER WINE PUNCH

4 bottles hock
1 bottle dry sherry
1.5 litres (2 1/2 pints) lemonade
ice cubes
2 mint sprigs
1 apple, quartered, cored and sliced
125 g (4 oz) strawberries (optional)

Mix the wine and sherry and divide between jugs. Top up with lemonade and ice cubes. Top with mint, apple and sliced strawberries if using.
Makes 30 glasses
NOTE: Any medium white wine may be used in place of hock.

Chocolate and Apricot Gâteau; Summer Wine Punch

BANANA ICE CREAM

450 ml (¾ pint)
 milk
175 g (6 oz) caster
 sugar
3 eggs, beaten
1 teaspoon vanilla
 essence
426 ml (15 fl oz)
 double cream
6 bananas, mashed

Put the milk, sugar and eggs in a small pan and heat gently, stirring constantly, until the mixture thickens. Strain into a bowl and add the vanilla essence. Leave to cool.

Whip the cream until slightly thickened and fold into the cooled custard. Stir in the mashed bananas. Pour into a rigid freezerproof container, cover, seal and freeze until firm.

Transfer to the refrigerator about 1 hour before serving to soften. Transfer to a chilled dish to serve. **Serves 20**

PEANUT BROWNIES

50 g (2 oz) cocoa
 powder
125 g (4 oz) butter,
 melted
250 g (8 oz) caster
 sugar
3 eggs, beaten
125 g (4 oz) self-
 raising flour, sifted
125 g (4 oz)
 unsalted peanuts,
 chopped

Stir the cocoa powder into the melted butter. Put the sugar, eggs, flour and peanuts into a mixing bowl, pour over the butter mixture and beat together thoroughly for 3 minutes.

Pour the mixture into a lined and greased oblong cake tin, 28 × 18 cm (11 × 7 inches). Bake in a preheated moderate oven, 180°C (350°F), Gas Mark 4, for 30 to 40 minutes until firm. Cut into 20 squares and cool. **Makes 20**

CIDER CUP

4.5 litres (8 pints)
 dry cider
1 × 1 litre (1.76
 pint) carton
 pineapple juice
1 litre (1¾ pints)
 lemonade
1 orange, sliced
1 lemon, sliced
1 tray ice cubes

Chill the cider, pineapple juice and lemonade separately. Just before serving, pour all three into a large bowl and float the orange and lemon slices and ice cubes on the top. **Makes about 40 glasses**
NOTE: Decorate individual servings with mint leaves if liked.

Banana Ice Cream; Peanut Brownies; Cider Cup

COCKTAIL PARTIES

Whatever the occasion and reason, whether it is a celebration for a business success, a friendly welcome to new arrivals in the neighbourhood or a thank you to friends for their help and support over the year, a cocktail party fits the bill.

In general, wine as well as a few well-chosen cocktails is served at a cocktail party and a choice here is also welcomed. There is nothing mystical about preparing cocktails although with such fancy names one could be forgiven for thinking so. All you require for making simple cocktails is a few basic pieces of equipment, the right liqueurs, spirits, mixers, decorations and a little imagination.

If you have a blender or food processor in your home then you can make virtually any cocktail – although a cocktail shaker for shaking and a mixing glass for stirring cocktails are preferable. Ice is a must – and plenty of it too – so an ice bucket makes a welcome aid. If crushed ice is required then wrap cubes in a clean tea towel and crush with a rolling pin or metal hammer.

Basic ingredients include a wide range of spirits, liqueurs, mixers, fruit and their juices. Other useful ingredients include Angostura bitters, coconut milk (cream or flesh), egg white, cream, Grenadine, ice cream and sugar syrup.

Food is usually kept to a minimum at such parties, since cocktails are usually taken before dinner, and the cocktail hour is usually between 6 and 8 pm or runs for 2 hours at most. A few well-chosen, colourful canapés, however, never go amiss. Dips and dunks with savoury crackers, crudités, olives, nuts and pastries are the order of the day, served chilled, warm or piping hot for contrast.

OLIVES ON HORSEBACK

30 large pimento-
 stuffed green olives
250 g (8 oz) mature
 Cheddar cheese,
 grated
10 streaky bacon
 rashers, derinded

Halve the olives lengthways and scoop out the pimento. Finely chop the pimento and mix thoroughly into the cheese. Stuff the olive halves with the cheese mixture and press the halves back together.

Stretch the bacon rashers with the back of a knife, then cut each rasher into 3 pieces. Wrap each stuffed olive in a piece of bacon and secure with a wooden cocktail stick.

Grill the olives for 4 to 5 minutes on each side or until the bacon is crisp.

Makes 30 olives

JAPANESE ALMONDS

625 g (1¼ lb)
 blanched almonds
50 g (2 oz) butter
2 tablespoons soy
 sauce
2 tablespoons dry
 sherry
½ teaspoon ground
 ginger
garlic salt

Spread the almonds in a shallow baking tin and toast in a preheated cool oven, 150°C (300°F), Gas Mark 2, for 20 minutes.

Meanwhile, melt the butter in a saucepan. Stir in the soy sauce, sherry and ginger. Pour over the almonds and continue toasting, stirring occasionally, for 15 to 20 minutes. Sprinkle with garlic salt to taste, then spread out on kitchen paper and leave to dry and cool.

Serves 12 to 16

SEEDED BISCUITS

24 water biscuits
50 g (2 oz) butter,
 melted
caraway, poppy or
 sesame seeds

Brush one side of each biscuit with melted butter. Sprinkle with caraway, poppy or sesame seeds and arrange the biscuits on baking sheets. Heat in a preheated moderate oven, 180°C (350°F), Gas Mark 4, for 5 minutes or until crisp and hot.

Makes 24 biscuits

LIPTOI

250 g (8 oz) curd
 cheese
250 g (8 oz) butter
½ teaspoon paprika
½ teaspoon caraway
 seeds
½ small onion,
 grated

Beat the ingredients together, adding more paprika and caraway seeds to taste. Serve with small savoury biscuits.

Serves 10 to 12

TUNA AND PARMESAN PUFFS

150 ml (¼ pint)
 water
50 g (2 oz) butter
75 g (3 oz) plain
 flour, sifted
2 eggs, beaten
25 g (1 oz) grated
 Parmesan cheese
FILLING:
1 × 198 g (7 oz) can
 tuna fish, drained
6 tablespoons
 mayonnaise
TO GARNISH:
parsley sprigs

Heat the water and butter slowly in a pan until the butter has melted. Remove from heat, quickly add all the flour and beat until the mixture leaves the side of the pan. Add the egg a little at a time, beating thoroughly between each addition. Beat in the cheese.

Spoon the mixture into a piping bag fitted with a 1 cm (½ inch) plain nozzle and pipe tiny mounds onto a dampened baking sheet, spacing them well apart. Bake in a preheated moderately hot oven, 200°C (400°F), Gas Mark 6, for 12 to 15 minutes, until crisp and golden.

Make a small slit in the side of each puff. Mash the tuna with the mayonnaise and spoon a little into each. Serve warm, garnished with parsley.

Makes about 150

Olives on Horseback; Japanese Almonds; Seeded Biscuits; Liptoi

SATAY WITH PEANUT SAUCE

350 g (12 oz) pork
    fillet
1 teaspoon chilli
    powder
1 teaspoon water
1 tablespoon oil
1 onion, grated
1 clove garlic, crushed
2 tablespoons lemon
    juice
5 tablespoons water
4 tablespoons crunchy
    peanut butter
1 teaspoon salt
1 teaspoon each
    ground cumin and
    coriander

Cut the pork fillet into small dice and thread 3 or 4 pieces on one end of wooden cocktail sticks. Cook under a preheated hot grill for 1 minute on each side or until cooked through. Drain on kitchen paper and keep warm.

Blend the chilli powder and 1 teaspoon water together to make a paste. Heat the oil in a pan, add the onion, garlic and chilli paste and fry gently until the onion is soft. Add the remaining ingredients, stirring well to combine. Transfer to a serving bowl.

Serve the satay with the sauce.

Makes about 20

NOTE: Garnish the satay with lemon slices and parsley if liked.

LAMB AND MINT MEATBALLS

500 g (1 lb) minced
    lamb
2 cloves garlic, crushed
2 teaspoons mint
    sauce
salt and pepper
1 egg, beaten
oil for shallow frying
PIQUANT DIP:
50 g (2 oz) demerara
    sugar
2 teaspoons cornflour
3 tablespoons water
4 tablespoons
    redcurrant jelly
2 tablespoons
    Worcestershire
    sauce
TO GARNISH:
parsley sprigs

Put the lamb in a bowl and add the garlic and mint sauce. Season well with salt and pepper and bind the mixture with the egg. With floured hands, roll into walnut-sized balls.

Heat the oil in a frying pan, add the meatballs in batches and fry for about 10 minutes until golden brown. Drain on kitchen paper and keep warm.

To make the dip, put the sugar, cornflour and water in a small pan and blend in the redcurrant jelly and Worcestershire sauce. Bring slowly to the boil and cook, stirring, until smooth.

Spear the meatballs onto cocktail sticks. Garnish with parsley and serve warm, with the dip.

Makes about 25

TAPENADE

150 g (5 oz) stuffed
    green olives
1 × 100 g (3½ oz)
    can tuna fish,
    drained
1 × 50 g (1¾ oz)
    can anchovies,
    drained
3 tablespoons capers
2 teaspoons lemon
    juice
150 ml (¼ pint)
    olive oil
1 tablespoon brandy
Dijon mustard
pepper

Reserve a few olives for garnish, slicing them finely. Put the rest of the olives and the remaining ingredients, with mustard and pepper to taste, in an electric blender and work until smooth.

Pour into a serving bowl and garnish with the sliced olives. Serve as a dip with Chive or Cheese Biscuits (see page 124).

Makes about 450 ml (¾ pint)

LEFT: *Satay with Peanut Sauce*
OPPOSITE: *Walnut Dip; Tapenade; Avocado and Cheese Dip; Sage Cream*

SAGE CREAM

125 g (4 oz) each
  Sage Derby and
  curd cheese
4 tablespoons natural
  yogurt
salt and pepper
green food colouring
  (optional)

Beat the ingredients together until smooth, with salt and pepper to taste, and a few drops of colouring if liked.

Serve as a dip; pipe onto Chive or Cheese Biscuits (see page 124) or into pieces of celery; or use to sandwich grape halves together.

Makes about 250 g (8 oz)

WALNUT DIP

125 g (4 oz) walnut
  pieces
1 clove garlic
1 tablespoon olive oil
1 teaspoon lemon
  juice
250 g (8 oz) natural
  yogurt
salt and pepper
1/4 cucumber, peeled

Put the walnut pieces, garlic, oil and lemon juice in an electric blender and work until smooth. Add the yogurt and blend in quickly. Season with salt and pepper to taste.

Transfer to a serving bowl. Chop the cucumber finely and stir into the dip. Serve chilled, with crisp fresh vegetables or biscuits.

Makes about 450 ml (3/4 pint)

AVOCADO AND CHEESE DIP

2 avocado pears
1 tablespoon lemon
  juice
2 tomatoes, skinned,
  seeded and chopped
2 cloves garlic, crushed
1/2 onion, grated
1 × 62.5 g (2.2 oz)
  packet creamy soft
  cheese
salt and pepper

Peel the avocados, halve and remove the stones, then mash with the lemon juice. Beat in the remaining ingredients, with salt and pepper to taste.

Serve as a dip with Chive or Cheese Biscuits (see page 124) or crisps.

Makes about 300 ml (1/2 pint)

SERVING SUGGESTIONS

The type of party you intend to give will unquestionably give a guide to party size. Thirty guests as a maximum is a good rule for a cocktail or wine party. Note that in this section, the cocktails serve one, unless otherwise stated.

Serve 6 to 8 different nibbles or dishes, some hot, some cold, with a varied selection of cocktails.

Make tee-total drinks all the more fun by serving in novelty containers including fruit shells like melon or pineapple, nut shells like coconut or small wooden bowls.

SPICED ALMONDS

3 tablespoons
  sunflower oil
125 g (4 oz) flaked
  almonds
1 teaspoon salt
1 teaspoon curry
  powder

Heat the oil in a frying pan, add the almonds and fry until golden brown. Drain on kitchen paper, then place in a serving dish. Mix the salt and curry powder together and sprinkle over the almonds; toss well to coat.
Makes 125 g (4 oz)

CHEESE BISCUITS

125 g (4 oz) plain
  flour
50 g (2 oz) butter
50 g (2 oz) Cheddar
  cheese, grated
1 egg yolk
2 teaspoons cold
  water

Sift the flour into a bowl. Rub in the butter until the mixture resembles breadcrumbs, then stir in the cheese. Add the egg yolk and water and mix to a firm dough.

Turn onto a lightly floured board, roll out to a 5 mm (¼ inch) thickness and cut into 3.5 cm (1½ inch) rounds with a plain cutter. Place well apart on greased baking sheets and bake in a preheated moderately hot oven, 200°C (400°F), Gas Mark 6, for 10 minutes. Cool on a wire rack.

Serve on their own or with dips, or use as a base for savoury spreads.
Makes about 50

CHIVE BISCUITS

125 g (4 oz) butter
2 × 62.5 g (2.2 oz)
  packets creamy soft
  cheese
125 g (4 oz) plain
  flour, sifted
1 tablespoon chopped
  chives

Cream the butter and cheese together until well blended. Stir in the flour and chives and mix with a fork until well combined. Roll the dough into a ball and wrap in cling film. Chill in the refrigerator for at least 1 hour.

Roll out to a 5 mm (¼ inch) thickness and cut into 3.5 cm (1½ inch) rounds with a plain cutter. Place well apart on greased baking sheets and bake in a preheated hot oven, 200°C (425°F), Gas Mark 7, for 10 minutes. Cool on a wire rack.

Serve on their own or with dips, or use as a base for savoury spreads.
Makes about 100

DEVILS ON HORSEBACK

25 g (1 oz) butter
1 onion, finely
  chopped
1 teaspoon dried sage
50 g (2 oz) fresh
  breadcrumbs
250 g (8 oz) prunes,
  stoned
10 streaky bacon
  rashers, derinded

Melt the butter in a pan, add the onion and fry gently until soft. Stir in the sage and breadcrumbs. Stuff the prunes with this mixture.

Stretch the bacon with the back of a knife, then cut each rasher in half. Wrap each prune in a piece of bacon and secure with a wooden cocktail stick. Grill for 4 to 5 minutes on each side, until the bacon is crisp.
Makes 20

CRUDITÉS

1 head of fennel
juice of ½ lemon
3-4 tomatoes, sliced
¼ cucumber, cut into
  strips
1 celery heart, sliced
½ small cauliflower,
  broken into florets
125 g (4 oz) broad
  beans
2 courgettes, sliced
1 red pepper, cored,
  seeded and sliced
1 green pepper, cored
  seeded and sliced
AIOLI:
4 cloves garlic
2 egg yolks
300 ml (½ pint)
  olive oil
salt and pepper
1-2 tablespoons wine
  vinegar
TO GARNISH:
chopped parsley
chopped chives

First, make the aioli (garlic mayonnaise): Crush the garlic in a mortar to a smooth paste. Add the egg yolks, one at a time, beating well with a wire whisk. Add the oil, drop by drop, whisking constantly until thickened, then add the remaining oil in a steady stream, whisking all the time. Add salt, pepper and vinegar to taste.

Cut the fennel into quarters and toss in the lemon juice. Arrange on a serving plate with the remaining vegetables.

Sprinkle the aioli with the parsley and chives. Serve with the vegetables.
Serves 4 to 6
NOTE: Any fresh, crisp vegetables may be used.

Spiced Almonds; Cheese Biscuits and Chive Biscuits piped with Sage Cream (see page 123); Devils on Horseback

MARTINI

1 measure gin
1 measure dry
vermouth

Shake the ingredients well with ice and strain into a cocktail glass. Decorate with a stuffed olive or a twist of lemon peel.

MARTINI DRY

2 measures gin
1 measure dry
vermouth

Shake the ingredients well with ice and strain into a cocktail glass. Decorate with a stuffed olive or a twist of lemon peel.

MARTINI EXTRA DRY

2 measures gin
1 dash of dry
vermouth

Shake the ingredients well with ice and strain into a cocktail glass. Decorate with a stuffed olive or a twist of lemon peel.

MARTINI SWEET

2 measures gin
1 measure sweet
vermouth

Shake the ingredients well with ice and strain into a cocktail glass. NOTE: For vodka martinis, simply substitute vodka for gin in any of the above martini recipes.

TOM COLLINS

juice of ½ lemon
1½ teaspoons caster
sugar
2 measures gin
soda water to top up

Shake the ingredients well with ice and strain into a tall tumbler. Add ice and a good dash of soda water. Decorate with lemon slices and cocktail cherries.

SILVER STREAK

1 measure kummel
1 measure gin

Shake the ingredients well with ice and strain into a cocktail glass.

WHITE LADY

½ measure lemon
  juice
½ measure
  Cointreau
1 measure gin

Shake the ingredients well with ice and strain into a cocktail glass. Decorate with an orange slice, speared with a cocktail cherry.

GIN FIX

1 tablespoon sugar
juice of ¼ lemon
1 measure water
2 measures gin

Fill a tall tumbler two-thirds full with crushed ice. Add all the ingredients and stir well. Decorate the rim of the glass with slices of any fruits in season.

GIN SLING

1 teaspoon sugar
2 measures gin
mineral or soda water
  to top up

Dissolve the sugar in a little water in a tall tumbler. Add the gin and a lump of ice. Top up with mineral water or soda water. Serve with straws.

THE FINISHING TOUCHES

The crowning glory of any cocktail has to be the decoration and here you can choose from the simple to the sumptuous. Any of the following will find a place in a comprehensive cocktail repertoire:

- Cherries, maraschino or glacé in red, green or yellow.
- Lemon, lime, orange and pineapple slices.
- Green olives, plain or stuffed for martinis.
- Citrus twists to place on the side of the glass and spirals of citrus peel to twist inside a glass.
- Celery leaves or sticks, pared cucumber peel and sprigs of mint or borage.
- Petite parasol umbrellas in a multitude of colours and designs.
- Melon wedges to position on the rim of the glass.
- Chocolate flakes to use as stirrers for chocolate-based drinks.
- Plain and coloured sugar crystals for frosting rims.
- Wafers to serve with creamy cocktails.
- Spices like cinnamon and nutmeg for dusting cocktails.

OPPOSITE: *Martini; Martini Dry; Martini Extra Dry; Martini Sweet*
ABOVE: *Tom Collins; Silver Streak; White Lady; Gin Fix*

DAIQUIRI

juice of ¼ lemon or
½ lime
2 measures dark rum
1 teaspoon caster sugar

Shake the ingredients well with ice and strain into a cocktail glass. Decorate with a cocktail cherry.

LITTLE DEVIL

½ measure lemon
juice
½ measure Cointreau
1 measure dark rum
1 measure gin

Shake the ingredients well with ice and strain into a cocktail glass.

PINA COLADA

3 measures dark rum
3 tablespoons coconut
milk
3 tablespoons crushed
pineapple

Place the ingredients in an electric blender. Add two cups of crushed ice and blend at high speed for 30 seconds. Strain into a tall tumbler and serve with a straw.

PARISIAN BLONDE

1 measure double
cream
little caster sugar
1 measure orange
Curaçao
1 measure dark rum

Shake the ingredients well with ice and strain into a cocktail glass. Decorate with orange slices.

CUBA LIBRE

2 measures dark rum
juice of ½ lime
coca-cola to top up

Half-fill a tumbler with ice cubes. Add the rum and lime juice and stir well. Top up with coca-cola and decorate with lime slices.

SCREWDRIVER

2 measures vodka
orange juice to top up

Pour the vodka over ice cubes in a tumbler and top up with orange juice. Stir well and decorate with orange slices.

BLOODY MARY

1 measure vodka
2 measures tomato
  juice
⅓ measure lemon
  juice
1 dash of Worcester-
  shire sauce
salt and pepper to
  taste

Shake the ingredients well with ice and strain into a wine glass. Garnish with celery leaves.

BLACK RUSSIAN

2 measures vodka
1 measure Kahlua

Pour the vodka and Kahlua over ice cubes in a whisky tumbler.
VARIATION: For a White Russian, top up with double cream. For a longer drink use a tall tumbler and top up with coca-cola.

HARVEY WALLBANGER

1 measure vodka
4 measures orange
  juice
½ measure Galliano

Pour the vodka and orange juice over ice cubes in a tall tumbler and stir well. Float the Galliano on top by pouring it over the back of a teaspoon onto the vodka and orange.

CORCOVADO

1 measure blue
  Curaçao
1 measure tequila
1 measure Drambuie
lemonade to top up

Shake the ingredients well with ice and strain into a tall tumbler filled with crushed ice. Top up with lemonade and decorate with a slice of lemon or lime. Serve with a straw.

TEQUILA SUNRISE

1¾ measures tequila
3½ measures orange
  juice
½ measure grenadine

Stir the tequila and orange juice with ice cubes in a shaker or jug and strain into a tall tumbler. Add ice cubes then slowly pour in the grenadine. Allow to settle, but stir once before drinking.

MARGARITA

1½ measures tequila
½ measure Cointreau
1 measure lemon or
  lime juice

Moisten the inner and outer edge of a cocktail glass with a slice of lemon or lime and dip in fine salt. Shake the ingredients well with ice and strain into the glass.

OPPOSITE: *Daiquiri; Little Devil; Pina Colada; Parisian Blonde*
RIGHT: *Tequila Sunrise*

ANGEL FACE

1 measure gin
1 measure apricot
  brandy
1 measure Calvados

Shake the ingredients well with ice and strain into a cocktail glass.

CORPSE REVIVER

½ measure sweet
  vermouth
½ measure Calvados
1 measure brandy

Shake the ingredients well with ice and strain into a cocktail glass.

STINGER

¼ measure white
  crème de menthe
¾ measure brandy

Shake the ingredients well with ice and strain into a cocktail glass.

BRANDY ALEXANDER

1 measure brandy
½ measure crème de
  cacao
1 measure double
  cream
little grated nutmeg

Shake the ingredients well with ice and strain into a wide champagne glass. Sprinkle with grated nutmeg.

MANHATTAN

1 dash of Angostura
  bitters
2 measures Canadian
  whisky
1 measure sweet
  vermouth

Shake the ingredients well with ice and strain into a cocktail glass.

Angel Face; Corpse Reviver; Stinger; Brandy Alexander

BETWEEN-THE-SHEETS

1 dash of lemon juice
1 measure brandy
1 measure Cointreau
1 measure dark rum

Shake the ingredients well with ice and strain into a cocktail glass.

BRANDY PUNCH

juice of 15 lemons
juice of 4 oranges
625 g (1¼ lb) caster sugar
300 ml (½ pint) orange Curaçao
2 measures grenadine
2.25 litres (4 pints) brandy
2.25 litres (4 pints) sparkling mineral water

Pour the fruit juices into a jug. Add the sugar and stir until dissolved. Place a large quantity of ice in a large punch bowl, add all the ingredients and stir well. Decorate with lemon and orange slices.
Serves 15 to 20

CHAMPAGNE CUP

1 tablespoon caster sugar
2 measures brandy
2 measures orange Curaçao
1 measure maraschino
1 measure Grand Marnier
1.2 litres (2 pints) Champagne

Put the ingredients into a large bowl. Add ice and stir well. Decorate with orange and pineapple slices.
Serves 4 to 6

CIDER CUP

1 measure maraschino
1 measure orange Curaçao
1 measure brandy
1.2 litres (2 pints) medium dry cider

Pour the ingredients into a large glass jug or bowl. Add ice and stir gently. Decorate with fruits in season.
Serves 4 to 6

Champagne Cup; Cider Cup

APPLEADE

2 large dessert apples
600 ml (1 pint)
    boiling water
½ teaspoon sugar

Chop the apples and place in a bowl. Pour the boiling water over the apples and add the sugar. Leave to stand for 10 minutes, then strain into a jug and allow to cool. Pour over ice cubes in a tall tumbler and decorate with an apple slice. Serve with a straw.
Serves 3

ANITA

1 measure orange
    juice
1 measure lemon juice
3 dashes of Angostura
    bitters
soda water to top up

Shake the ingredients well with ice. Strain into a tumbler and top up with soda water. Decorate with lemon and orange slices. Serve with a straw.

SAN FRANCISCO

1 measure orange
    juice
1 measure lemon juice
1 measure pineapple
    juice
1 measure grapefruit
    juice
2 dashes of grenadine
1 egg white
soda water to top up

Shake the ingredients well with ice and strain into a wine glass. Top up with soda water and decorate with fruit slices speared onto a cocktail stick. Serve with a straw.

CARIB CREAM

1 small banana,
    chopped
1 measure lemon juice
1 measure milk
1 teaspoon finely
    chopped walnuts

Place the banana, lemon juice and milk in an electric blender with some crushed ice and blend on maximum speed until smooth. Pour into a cocktail glass and sprinkle the chopped walnuts on top just before serving.

Appleade; Anita

TENDERBERRY

6-8 strawberries
1 measure grenadine
1 measure double
  cream
1 measure dry ginger
  ale
little ground ginger

Place the strawberries, grenadine and cream in an electric blender with some crushed ice and blend on maximum speed for 30 seconds. Pour into a tumbler. Add the dry ginger and stir. Sprinkle a little ginger on top and decorate with a strawberry, if liked.

CAFÉ ASTORIA

1½ measures coffee
  essence
2 measures milk
¼ measure pineapple
  juice
¼ measure lemon
  juice
chocolate sugar
  strands to decorate

Place the ingredients in an electric blender with some crushed ice and blend on maximum speed for 30 seconds. Pour into a cocktail glass and sprinkle sugar strands on top just before serving.

TEMPERANCE MOCKTAIL

2 measures lemon
  juice
2 dashes of grenadine
1 egg yolk

Shake the ingredients well with ice and strain into a cocktail glass. Decorate with a cocktail cherry.

COOL PASSION

1 × 500 ml (17.6 fl
  oz) carton orange
  and passionfruit
  juice
1 × 1 litre (1.76
  pint) carton
  pineapple juice
1 × 1½ litre (50 fl oz)
  bottle lemonade
crushed ice

Pour the two fruit juices into a large jug and stir well to mix.
  Just before serving, stir in the lemonade. Pour into glasses containing a little crushed ice.
Makes about 20 glasses

Carib Cream; Café Astoria; Temperance Mocktail

CHILDREN'S PARTIES

Toddler, tiny tot or teenage, bonfire, barbecue or birthday, there is a children's party to suit every occasion and every age group. Perhaps the most fun to organise, you can let your imagination run wild with ideas for party themes, novelty cakes and decorations.

First decide upon your party theme – a pirates', Arabian, Caribbean or nursery rhyme character are options. The theme will influence the food you cook, the decorations required, the novelty cake to make, and the ideal numbers to invite.

Forward planning is the key to success so make a list at the outset and spend a few hours shopping for the food and accessories you'll need – including paper plates, cups, straws, streamers, napkins, candles for the cake and any novelty gifts.

Children appreciate food that is small, dainty, attractive and flavourful – small cocktail sausages, petite sandwiches, crisps and small savouries are enormously popular at almost any age.

The recipes on pages 140 to 143 provide the ideal party menu for 12 tiny tots aged between 3 and 5 years old. In general, this age group is far more interested in the food than any party games.

Over 5 years old and the reverse is often the case, so put your efforts into planning a party with lots of activity. The recipes on pages 136 to 139 provide the ideal party menu for 4 to 8-year-old children at Christmas and serve 12 comfortably. The Christmas tree cake on page 138 makes a splendid centrepiece.

All children love a bonfire party and it is the ideal choice for an autumn birthday. Served indoors or out, the recipes on pages 144 to 147 will cope with 14 children aged between say 8 and 12 years old.

PORCUPINES

2 oranges or
  grapefruit
150 g (5 oz) Cheddar
  cheese, cubed
1 × 227 g (8 oz) can
  pineapple pieces,
  drained
50 cocktail sticks
2 stuffed olives,
  halved crosswise
1 small gherkin,
  halved
20 cocktail sausages,
  grilled

Cut a slice off one side of each fruit so they will stand firmly.

Thread cheese and pineapple onto cocktail sticks, and stick into one fruit to make the porcupine's spikes.

Pierce 2 olive halves and 1 gherkin piece with halved cocktail sticks. Push them into the fruit to make the porcupine's eyes and nose.

Place a sausage on each of the remaining cocktail sticks and stick them into the other fruit. Make the eyes and nose in the same way.

Makes 2 'porcupines'

PINEAPPLE ORANGE DRINK

4 oranges
50 g (2 oz) caster
  sugar
1.2 litres (2 pints)
  boiling water
600 ml (1 pint)
  pineapple juice
orange slices to decorate

Finely grate the rind from the oranges and place in a heatproof jug. Add the sugar and water and stir until the sugar has dissolved. Squeeze the juice from the oranges and strain into the jug. Cool, then add the pineapple juice; chill. Serve topped with orange slices.

Makes 2 litres (3½ pints)

CHESSBOARD SANDWICHES

8 slices brown bread
8 slices white bread
FILLINGS:
50 g (2 oz) butter
6 tablespoons
  mayonnaise
3 hard-boiled eggs,
  finely chopped
50 g (2 oz) cream
  cheese
75 g (3 oz) Cheddar
  cheese, grated
2 tablespoons
  chopped chives
salt and pepper

For the fillings, beat the butter with the mayonnaise; divide in half. Stir the chopped eggs into one portion; mix the cheeses and chives into the other portion. Season both with salt and pepper to taste.

Make the sandwiches using one slice of brown bread, one slice of white and one filling for each. Remove the crusts, then cut each sandwich into 4 squares.

Arrange them in two layers on a square cake board, alternating the brown and white sides to create a chessboard effect.

Makes 32

MARMITE BITES

215 g (7½ oz)
  packet frozen puff
  pastry, thawed
1 tablespoon marmite
½ teaspoon water

Roll out the pastry thinly on a floured surface to a rectangle about 25 × 30 cm (10 × 12 inches). Mix the marmite and water together and spread over the pastry to cover completely. Roll up loosely from the shorter side like a Swiss roll; position the join underneath. Chill for 20 minutes.

Cut into 5 mm (¼ inch) slices, place on baking sheets and make a slit in each from edge to centre. Bake in a pre-heated moderately hot oven, 200°C (400°F), Gas Mark 6, for 10 minutes or until golden. Serve warm or cold.

Makes about 30

COLA FLOAT

1.75 litres (3 pints)
  cola
12 scoops vanilla
  easy scoop ice cream

Three-quarters fill 12 beakers with cola, then place a scoop of ice cream on top. Serve with straws.

Serves 12

LEFT: *Cola Float; Chessboard Sandwiches*

CELERY BOATS

113 g (4 oz) cream
  cheese
1 tablespoon chopped
  chives
salt and pepper
1 head of celery,
  divided into sticks
TO FINISH:
rice paper
cocktail sticks
shredded lettuce

Place the cheese in a bowl with the chives and salt and pepper to taste. Mix well until smooth. Spoon a little of the mixture into each celery stick and spread smoothly. Cut into 6 cm (2½ inch) lengths. Cut the rice paper into triangles, spear with a cocktail stick and stick into the celery.

Arrange the lettuce on a serving dish and place the celery boats on top.
Makes about 20

TUNA TUGS

1 × 198 g (7 oz) can
  tuna fish, drained
50 g (2 oz) soft
  margarine
3 tablespoons
  mayonnaise
salt and pepper
12 small bridge rolls,
  halved
¼ cucumber
1 carrot
24 strips cucumber
  peel (optional)

Place the tuna fish in a bowl and mash with a fork. Add the margarine, mayonnaise, and salt and pepper to taste. Mix with a fork until smooth. Place 2 teaspoons of the mixture on each half roll and smooth to the edges.

Cut the cucumber into 1 cm (½ inch) sticks and place vertically on each roll. Cut the carrot into 2.5 cm (1 inch) sticks and place in front of the cucumber as funnels. Wrap the cucumber peel around the tugs, if using.
Makes 24

FUN FOOD

Without doubt the most important thing to bear in mind when preparing food for a children's party is that the food must look attractive – small appetites need stimulating when there are busy party games to play!

This is never more true than with savouries so cut out sandwiches using animal cutters, arrange in a chessboard effect or roll up then slice Swiss roll style. Set sail celery boats on a sea of shredded lettuce. Add nibbles like vegetable sticks and chipolatas stuck into fruit for a porcupine effect.

Sweet offerings like ice cream and jelly need little enticement but will look all the more attractive if scooped and decorated like a clown or set in a special mould.

Drinks can also be given the 5 star treatment with straws, citrus slices or even a fizzy float of ice cream.

Celery Boats; Tuna Tugs; Marmite Bites

Christmas Tree

ICE CREAM CLOWNS

2 litres (3½ pints)
  vanilla easy scoop
  ice cream
60 smarties
12 liquorice comfits
12 jelly beans
2 tablespoons
  chocolate sugar
  strands
2 tablespoons leftover
  butter icing (see
  page 150)
12 ice cream cones
12 chocolate biscuits

Chill a baking sheet in the freezer for 10 minutes. Using a large ice cream scoop, make 12 ice cream balls. Arrange them on the baking sheet and return to the freezer for 1 hour.

Working quickly, press on smarties for eyes and comfits for nose and mouth. Return to freezer for 3 hours.

Spread icing around the top of each ice cream cone and dip in chocolate strands. Put 3 dots of icing on each cone and stick a smartie on each one. Arrange the biscuits on a serving dish and place an ice cream ball on each. Top with an ice cream cone 'clown's hat' and serve immediately.
Makes 12

MERINGUE MUSHROOMS

2 egg whites
125 g (4 oz) caster
  sugar
1 lime jelly
3 tablespoons double
  cream, whipped
25 g (1 oz) plain
  chocolate, grated

Whisk the egg whites until stiff, then whisk in 2 tablespoons of the sugar. Carefully fold in the remaining sugar.

Spoon the mixture into a piping bag fitted with a 1 cm (½ inch) plain nozzle. Line a baking sheet with non-stick paper and pipe 5 cm (2 inch) meringue mounds for the mushroom heads, and 2 cm (¾ inch) mounds for stalks. Bake in a preheated very cool oven, 110°C (225°F), Gas Mark ¼, for about 2 hours, until crisp and dry. Allow to cool.

Meanwhile, make up the jelly with 450 ml (¾ pint) boiling water, as directed on the packet. When set firmly, turn onto a sheet of grease-proof paper and chop finely. Spread on a large plate to represent grass.

Scoop out a hollow with a sharp knife on the underside of the larger meringues. Place a little cream in each hollow and attach the 'stalks'. Sprinkle over the chocolate and arrange the mushrooms on the 'grass'.
Makes 10 to 12

CHRISTMAS TREE

4-egg Victoria sand-
  wich cake mixture
  (see page 150)
375 g (12 oz) butter
  icing (see page 150)
125 g (4 oz) apricot
  glaze (see page 150)
red, yellow and green
  food colourings
1 star, cut from
  marzipan
silver balls
smarties
liquorice comfits
candles in holders

Turn the cake mixture into two 20 × 30 cm (8 × 12 inch) Swiss roll tins. Bake in a preheated moderate oven, 180°C (350°F), Gas Mark 4, for 20 to 25 minutes; cool on a wire rack.

Sandwich the cakes together with a quarter of the icing. Cut to tree shape (see diagram) attaching 2 cut out pieces to the top. Stick 2 other cut pieces together with a little icing and shape to form the tub.

Brush cut edges with apricot glaze and leave to dry. Colour one quarter of the icing red, 2 tablespoons yellow and the remainder green. Spread the green icing over the tree, then fork up.

Spread the red icing over the tub, attach to the tree and pipe yellow rosettes around the tub. Stick on the star, silver balls, sweets and candles.
Makes one Christmas tree

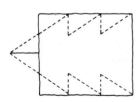

CHERRY MINCE PIES

125 g (4 oz)
    shortcrust pastry
    (see page 150)
FILLING:
175 g (6 oz)
    mincemeat
50 g (2 oz)
    maraschino
    cherries, drained
    and quartered
1 teaspoon lemon
    juice
MERINGUE:
1 egg white
50 g (2 oz) caster
    sugar
TO DECORATE:
3 maraschino cherries,
    quartered

Roll out the pastry thinly on a floured surface and use to line twelve 7.5 cm (3 inch) patty tins. Prick the bases well and chill for 15 minutes.

Press a piece of foil into each pastry case and bake in a preheated moderately hot oven, 200°C (400°F), Gas Mark 6 for 10 to 15 minutes. Remove the foil and return to the oven for 2 minutes.

Mix filling ingredients together. Divide between the pastry cases.

Whisk the egg white until stiff, then whisk in the sugar a tablespoon at a time. Spoon into a piping bag fitted with a 1 cm (½ inch) fluted nozzle and pipe a rosette on top of each pie. Top with the cherry pieces.

Bake in a preheated moderate oven, 180°C (350°F), Gas Mark 4, for 6 minutes. Serve warm or cold.
Makes 12

GINGERBREAD PEOPLE

125 g (4 oz) plain
    flour
½ teaspoon
    bicarbonate of soda
½ teaspoon ground
    ginger
½ teaspoon ground
    cinnamon
25 g (1 oz) butter or
    margarine
50 g (2 oz) soft
    brown sugar
2 tablespoons golden
    syrup
1 teaspoon milk
50 g (2 oz) stiff glacé
    icing (see page
    150)

Sift the flour, soda and spices into a bowl. Place the fat, sugar and syrup in a pan over low heat until melted. Cool, then mix into the flour with the milk to make a firm dough. Wrap in polythene and chill for 30 minutes.

Turn the dough onto a floured surface and roll out to a 5 mm (¼ inch) thickness. Using gingerbread cutters, cut out 12 figures and place on greased baking sheets.

Bake in a preheated moderate oven, 160°C (325°F), Gas Mark 3, for 10 to 15 minutes, until firm. Transfer to a wire rack to cool.

Spoon the icing into a greaseproof paper piping bag fitted with a writing nozzle and pipe eyes, nose, mouth, buttons and borders on each figure.
Makes 12

Chocolate Nuggets; Cherry Mince Pies; Gingerbread People

CHOCOLATE NUGGETS

50 g (2 oz)
    margarine
175 g (6 oz) plain
    chocolate
2 tablespoons clear
    honey
250 g (8 oz)
    digestive biscuits,
    crushed
16 smarties

Place the margarine, chocolate and honey in a saucepan and heat gently until melted. Stir in the biscuit crumbs and mix thoroughly.

Turn into a greased and lined shallow 18 cm (7 inch) square cake tin and smooth the top. Mark into squares with a sharp knife and place a smartie in the centre of each. Leave to set, then cut into squares.
Makes 16

CHEESE TWIGS

125 g (4 oz) plain
    flour
pinch of salt
50 g (2 oz) butter or
    margarine
75 g (3 oz) Cheddar
    cheese, coarsely
    grated
1 Oxo cube, roughly
    crumbled
1 egg yolk
2-3 teaspoons water

Sift the flour and salt into a bowl. Rub in the fat until the mixture resembles breadcrumbs. Stir in the cheese and Oxo cube, then add the egg yolk and enough water to mix to a firm dough.

Turn onto a floured surface and knead lightly. Roll out thinly into a large square, about 5 mm (¼ inch) thick. Cut into strips 5 mm (¼ inch) wide and 7.5 cm (3 inches) long.

Place on baking sheets and bake in a preheated moderately hot oven, 200°C (400°F), Gas Mark 6, for 8 to 10 minutes, until golden.
Makes about 80

EGG AND BACON TARTLETS

125 g (4 oz)
    shortcrust pastry
    (see page 150)
75 g (3 oz) streaky
    bacon, derinded
    and chopped
1 large egg
5 tablespoons milk
25 g (1 oz) Cheddar
    cheese, grated
salt and pepper
pinch of dry mustard

Roll out the dough thinly on a floured surface and use to line twelve 7.5 cm (3 inch) patty tins; chill for 15 minutes.

Place the bacon in a small pan and fry gently in its own fat until beginning to turn golden. Beat the egg and milk together in a bowl, beat in the cheese, then stir in the bacon. Season with salt, pepper and mustard to taste. Divide between pastry cases.

Bake in a preheated moderately hot oven, 200°C (400°F), Gas Mark 6, for 15 to 20 minutes, until set and golden.
Makes 12

SANDWICH HOUSE

10 large slices brown
    bread
20-30 cheese twigs
    (see above)
1 celery stick, cut into
    thin strips
1 teaspoon chopped
    parsley
parsley sprigs
1 carrot
1-2 teaspoons cream
    cheese
FILLING:
25 g (1 oz) soft
    margarine
50 g (2 oz) cream
    cheese
1 × 120 g (4¼ oz)
    can sardines in
    tomato sauce
salt and pepper

For the filling, beat the margarine with the cream cheese, sardines and their sauce, and salt and pepper to taste. Use to make up 5 rounds of sandwiches and remove the crusts.

Cut 2 rounds into 6 oblongs. Place the 2 cut rounds on top of each other on a cake board to make an oblong.

Cut the remaining sandwiches into 12 triangles. Place 8 triangles on top of the oblong to form a roof. Arrange the cheese twigs along either side.

Cut the remaining bread triangles in half and arrange in front as a fence. Lay the celery in the 'garden' and sprinkle with chopped parsley to represent grass. Position parsley sprigs for bushes.

Cut pieces of carrot for the door, windows and chimney. Use a small fluted cutter to make carrot flowers. Use a little cream cheese to stick on the door and windows; place a blob on the chimney to represent smoke.
Serves 8
NOTE: Use any fillings you like for this house: marmite, peanut butter and sandwich spreads are all popular.

CHOCOLATE MILK

125 g (4 oz) plain
    chocolate, chopped
150 ml (¼ pint)
    boiling water
900 ml (1½ pints)
    milk

Place the chocolate and water in an electric blender or food processor and blend on maximum speed for 10 seconds. Add the milk and blend for a further 10 seconds. Allow to cool, then chill. Serve with straws.
Makes about 1.2 litres (2 pints)

PARTY DECORATIONS

Whether you're giving a tiny tot's first birthday party or informal hallowe'en, the way in which you decorate a children's party celebration will undoubtedly play a large part in your reputation as a good party-giver.

Paper tablecloths and napkins are a must at children's parties and are often more attractive too when you can choose from Disney to Spacewars as your theme. Scatter with streamers, balloons, whistles and other novelties.

Table decorations are also important, especially for feast days. Set the scene at hallowe'en with mini broomsticks, witches' hats, skeletons, black cats and apple bobbing tubs. At Christmas opt for crackers, holly, novelty snowmen, father Christmases, angels and baubles.

Candles, placed in bottles and set deep into the earth in flower borders, or special outdoor flame torches, provide interesting lighting for bonfire parties. Alternatively, hollow out and light pumpkins with candles then hang lantern-style in the garden.

Cheese Twigs; Sandwich House; White Mice; Marshmallow Tarts

PINWHEEL SANDWICHES

4 slices medium sliced
  brown bread, crusts
  removed
FILLING:
75 g (3 oz) cream
  cheese
1 tablespoon
  mayonnaise
salt and pepper
1 celery stick

For the filling, beat the cream cheese with the mayonnaise and salt and pepper to taste. Cut the celery into four 5 mm (¼ inch) sticks, the same length as the bread. Roll out the bread lightly with a rolling pin and spread thickly with the cheese filling. Place a stick of celery across one end of each slice. Roll up tightly, pressing the edge down firmly. Wrap in cling film and chill until required.

Cut the rolls into 1 cm (½ inch) slices to serve.

Makes about 32

FRUIT JELLY RABBIT

1 raspberry jelly
1 banana
50 g (2 oz) grapes,
  halved and pipped
50 g (2 oz)
  raspberries

Make up the jelly with 450 ml (¾ pint) boiling water (or as directed on the packet) and allow to cool.

Slice the banana and add to the jelly with the grapes and raspberries. Turn into a 750 ml (1¼ pint) rabbit mould and leave to set. Dip quickly into hot water to unmould.

Serves 6 to 8

NOTE: To serve more children, make up a lime jelly. Allow to set, then chop finely. Arrange around the rabbit to represent grass.

LEMONADE

4 lemons
75 g (3 oz) caster
  sugar
1.2 litres (2 pints)
  boiling water

Finely grate the rind from the lemons and place in a heatproof jug with the sugar. Pour over the water and stir until the sugar has dissolved. Squeeze the juice from the lemons and strain into the jug. Allow to cool, then chill.

Makes 1.5 litres (2½ pints)

WHITE MICE

2 egg whites
125 g (4 oz) caster
  sugar
24 split almonds
36 coloured 'silver'
  balls
few red liquorice
  bootlaces, cut into
  10 cm (4 inch)
  lengths

Whisk the egg whites until stiff and dry looking. Whisk in the sugar, a tablespoon at a time, and continue whisking until very thick.

Spoon into a piping bag fitted with a 1 cm (½ inch) plain nozzle. Line a baking sheet with non-stick paper and pipe the mixture into mounds, wide at one end and tapering off to a point at the other; neaten with a palette knife if necessary. Place the almonds in the tapered end for ears. Position the balls for eyes and nose.

Bake in a preheated very cool oven, 110°C (225°F), Gas Mark ¼, for 2 hours. Cool on the baking sheets.

Make a small hole in the tail end of each mouse with a skewer and stick in a piece of liquorice to make a tail.

Makes 12

Pinwheel Sandwiches

MARSHMALLOW TARTS

*125 g (4 oz)
    shortcrust pastry
    (see page 150)*
*2 tablespoons
    raspberry jam*
*2 tablespoons apricot
    jam*
*12 pink and white
    marshmallows*
*3 glacé cherries,
    quartered*

Roll out the pastry thinly on a floured surface and use to line twelve 7.5 cm (3 inch) patty tins. Chill for 15 minutes.

Place a teaspoon of jam in each pastry case. Bake in a preheated moderately hot oven, 200°C (400°F), Gas Mark 6, for 10 to 15 minutes, until the pastry is golden.

Place a pink marshmallow on the raspberry tarts and a white one on the apricot tarts. Return to the oven for 1 minute to melt the marshmallow slightly. Transfer to a wire rack to cool. Place a piece of cherry in the centre of each tart.
Makes 12

Smartie Buns

SMARTIE BUNS

*50 g (2 oz) soft
    margarine*
*50 g (2 oz) caster
    sugar*
*50 g (2 oz) self-
    raising flour, sifted*
*pinch of baking
    powder*
1 egg
TOPPING:
*50 g (2 oz) glacé
    icing (see page 150)*
*selection of food
    colourings*
24 smarties

Place the cake ingredients in a mixing bowl and beat vigorously for 2 minutes, until thoroughly blended.

Arrange 24 petits fours cases on a baking sheet and two-thirds fill with mixture. Bake in a preheated moderate oven, 180°C (350°F), Gas Mark 4, for 15 minutes. Cool on a wire rack.

Divide the icing into several portions and colour each one with a few drops of colouring. Spoon a little icing onto the centre of each cake and top with a smartie.
Makes 24

TRAFFIC LIGHT BISCUITS

*25 g (1 oz) caster
    sugar*
*50 g (2 oz) butter or
    margarine*
*75 g (3 oz) plain
    flour, sifted*
TOPPING:
*50 g (2 oz) glacé
    icing (see page
    150)*
*few drops each of red,
    yellow and green
    food colouring*
1 tablespoon red jam

Beat the sugar and fat together until light and fluffy. Add the flour and mix until the mixture binds together.

Turn onto a floured surface and knead until smooth. Roll out to an oblong 4 mm (¼ inch) thick and cut into 2.5 × 7.5 cm (1 × 3 inch) strips. Cut out 3 circles with a 1.5 cm (¾ inch) pastry cutter or piping nozzle from each of half the strips.

Place all the strips on baking sheets and bake in a preheated moderate oven, 160°C (325°F), Gas Mark 3, for 15 to 20 minutes, until pale golden. Leave to cool on the baking sheets.

Divide the icing into 3 portions and colour each with a food colouring. Spread the plain biscuits thinly with jam. Place the biscuits with holes in on top. Fill the holes with the coloured icing to represent the traffic lights.
Makes about 9

CHOCOLATE ROCKS

*2 tablespoons clear
    honey*
25g (1oz) margarine
*125 g (4 oz) plain
    chocolate*
*125 g (4 oz) bran
    flakes*

Place the honey, margarine and chocolate in a pan and stir over a low heat until melted. Add the bran flakes and mix thoroughly until well coated. Spoon into paper cases and leave to set.
Makes about 15

CORN RELISH

4 tomatoes, skinned
  and chopped
1 onion, chopped
1 celery stick, chopped
4 tablespoons brown
  sugar
4 tablespoons malt
  vinegar
½ teaspoon mustard
  powder
salt and pepper
2 teaspoons cornflour
1 × 198 g (7 oz) can
  sweetcorn, drained

Place the tomatoes, onion, celery, sugar, vinegar, mustard, and salt and pepper to taste, in an enamel pan and simmer for 15 minutes.

Blend the cornflour with 2 tablespoons water and stir into the sauce with the sweetcorn. Bring to the boil, stirring occasionally, and boil until thickened. Leave to cool, then serve with Hamburgers, Crispy Sausages and Frankfurter and Bacon Rolls.

Makes 600 ml (1 pint)

HAMBURGERS

1.5 kg (3½ lb)
  ground beef
2 large onions, finely
  chopped
4 tablespoons
  chopped parsley
1 tablespoon salt
2 tablespoons Worcester-
  shire sauce
pepper
14 hamburger buns
3 dill cucumbers,
  sliced lengthways
1 onion, thinly sliced

Mix the beef, onions, parsley, salt, sauce, and pepper to taste in a large bowl until thoroughly combined. Divide into 14 portions and shape each into a flat round about 2 cm (¾ inch) thick. Cook under a preheated hot grill for 3 minutes on each side.

Slice the buns in half and place a hamburger on the bottom half of each. Top with a few slices of dill cucumber and onion and cover with the top half of the bun. Serve with Corn Relish (see above).

Makes 14

FRANKFURTER ROLLS

14 frankfurters
4 processed cheese
  slices
14 rashers streaky
  bacon, derinded
14 bridge rolls, split
  open

Make a cut along each frankfurter, two thirds of the way through. Cut each slice of cheese into 4 strips and place one in each frankfurter.

Stretch the bacon with a palette knife and wind one rasher around each frankfurter to cover the cheese.

Cook under a preheated hot grill for 5 minutes, turning occasionally.

Place a frankfurter inside each roll.

Serves 14

HALLOWE'EN SOUP

2 tablespoons oil
2 onions, chopped
2 carrots, chopped
2 celery sticks,
    chopped
250 g (8 oz) swede,
    chopped
2 × 397 g (14 oz)
    cans tomatoes
1 tablespoon tomato
    purée
2 teaspoons salt
1 teaspoon soft brown
    sugar
1.5 litres (2½ pints)
    water
1 bouquet garni
pepper

Heat the oil in a large pan, add the onions and fry until softened. Stir in the carrots, celery, swede and the tomatoes with their juice.

Add the remaining ingredients, seasoning with pepper to taste. Bring to the boil, cover and simmer for 40 minutes, until the vegetables are tender. Cool slightly, remove the bouquet garni, then work in an electric blender or food processor until smooth. Serve hot, in mugs.
Makes 2.25 litres (4 pints)

CRISPY SAUSAGES

450 g (1 lb)
    chipolata sausages
4 tablespoons peanut
    butter
1 tablespoon French
    mustard
2-3 tablespoons water
16 thin slices brown
    bread, crusts
    removed
50 g (2 oz) soft
    margarine

Grill the sausages under a preheated hot grill, turning frequently, until browned all over. Put the peanut butter and mustard in a bowl, add the water and mix thoroughly. Roll the bread lightly with a rolling pin, then spread with the peanut mixture.

Place a sausage diagonally across each slice of bread and roll up tightly, securing with a cocktail stick. Spread each roll with margarine and place on a baking sheet. Bake in a preheated moderately hot oven, 200°C (400°F), Gas Mark 6, for 15 to 20 minutes, until golden. Serve with Corn Relish (see opposite).
Makes 16
NOTE: Butter may be used instead of peanut butter, in which case omit the water.

HOT BLACKCURRANT PUNCH

300 ml (½ pint)
    blackcurrant health
    drink
300 ml (½ pint)
    orange juice
1 teaspoon ground
    cinnamon
2.25 litres (4 pints)
    boiling water
1 orange, thinly
    sliced

Place the blackcurrant and orange juices in a large heatproof jug. Blend the cinnamon with a little of the boiling water, then add to the jug with the remaining water. Float the orange slices on top. Serve in mugs.
Makes 2.75 litres (5 pints)

RIGHT: *Hot Blackcurrant Punch; Hallowe'en Soup; Crispy Sausages*
OPPOSITE: *Corn Relish; Hamburgers; Frankfurter Rolls*

BONFIRE FIZZ

1.2 litres (2 pints)
    ginger beer
250 ml (8 fl oz)
    lemon squash
600 ml (1 pint) soda
    water
1 lemon, thinly sliced

Place the ginger beer and lemon squash in a large jug. Top up with the soda water and float the lemon slices on top.
Makes 2 litres (3½ pints)

CHOCOLATE FUDGE CAKES

125 g (4 oz) plain
    chocolate
300 ml (½ pint)
    milk
125 g (4 oz) soft
    brown sugar
125 g (4 oz) butter
    or margarine
125 g (4 oz) caster
    sugar
2 eggs, separated
250 g (8 oz) plain
    flour
1 teaspoon
    bicarbonate of soda
CHOCOLATE FUDGE
    ICING:
25 g (1 oz) butter or
    margarine
1-2 tablespoons milk
125 g (4 oz) icing
    sugar
1 tablespoon cocoa
    powder

Line and grease an 18 × 28 cm (7 × 11 inch) baking tin, allowing the paper to come 2.5 cm (1 inch) above 2 opposite sides.

Place the chocolate, 4 tablespoons of the milk and the brown sugar in a pan and heat gently, stirring, until melted. Stir in the remaining milk.

Cream the fat and caster sugar until light and fluffy, then beat in the egg yolks thoroughly.

Sift the flour and bicarbonate of soda together. Add to the creamed mixture with the chocolate mixture and beat until smooth. Whisk the egg whites until soft peaks form. Fold 1 tablespoon into the mixture to lighten it, then carefully fold in the rest.

Turn into the prepared tin and bake in a preheated moderate oven, 180°C (350°F), Gas Mark 4, for 50 minutes, until the cake springs back when lightly pressed. Turn onto a wire rack to cool slightly.

To make the icing, place the fat and 1 tablespoon milk in a small pan and heat gently until melted. Sift the icing sugar and cocoa together and add to the pan, mixing well until smooth; add a little more milk if necessary.

Pour over the warm cake and spread evenly to the edges. Allow to set completely, then cut into squares.
Makes 15

CARAMEL SQUARES

125 g (4 oz) butter
    or margarine
50 g (2 oz) caster
    sugar
125 g (4 oz) plain
    flour
50 g (2 oz) ground
    rice
CARAMEL FILLING:
125 g (4 oz) butter
    or margarine
50 g (2 oz) caster
    sugar
2 tablespoons golden
    syrup
1 × 196 g (6.1 oz)
    can condensed milk
TOPPING:
125 g (4 oz) plain
    chocolate
2 tablespoons milk

Cream the fat and sugar together until light and fluffy. Add the flour and rice and stir until the mixture binds together. Knead until smooth.

Roll out to a square and press evenly into a shallow 20 cm (8 inch) square tin; prick well. Bake in a preheated moderate oven, 180°C (350°F), Gas Mark 4, for 30 minutes. Cool in the tin.

Place the filling ingredients in a pan and heat gently, stirring until dissolved. Bring slowly to the boil, then cook, stirring, for 5 to 7 minutes, until golden. Spread over the biscuit mixture and leave to set.

For the topping, place the chocolate and milk in a small pan and heat gently until melted. Spread over the biscuits and leave to set. Cut into squares to serve.
Makes 16

Bonfire Fizz; Chocolate Fudge Cakes; Caramel Squares

MINT ICE CREAM CORNETS

MINT ICE CREAM:
3 egg yolks
150 g (5 oz) caster sugar
300 ml (½ pint) milk
1 tablespoon gelatine, dissolved in 3 tablespoons water
6 drops green food colouring
1 teaspoon peppermint essence
1 × 410 g (14.5 oz) can evaporated milk, chilled

TO SERVE:
14 ice cream cornets
7 chocolate flakes, halved

To make the ice cream: place the egg yolks and sugar in a heatproof bowl and beat until pale and creamy. Bring the milk almost to the boil, pour onto the egg mixture and mix thoroughly.

Place the bowl over a pan of simmering water and stir until thickened. Add the gelatine and stir until dissolved. Strain, allow to cool, then stir in the colouring and essence. Leave until just beginning to set.

Whisk the evaporated milk until thick, then whisk in the custard. Turn into a rigid freezerproof container, cover, seal and freeze until firm.

Transfer to the refrigerator 30 minutes before serving to soften. Scoop into the cornets and stick half a chocolate flake in each.
Makes 14

Mint Ice Cream Cornets; Toffee Apples; Popcornets

TOFFEE APPLES

14 short wooden sticks or skewers
14 medium dessert apples
750 g (1½ lb) demerara sugar
75 g (3 oz) butter
2 teaspoons vinegar
175 ml (6 fl oz) water
2 tablespoons golden syrup

Push a stick firmly into the core of each apple.

Heat the remaining ingredients gently in a large heavy-based pan until the sugar has dissolved. Bring to the boil and boil for 5 minutes without stirring, until 143°C (290°F) is registered on a sugar thermometer, or until a little mixture dropped into cold water forms a hard ball; brush sides of the pan with a brush dipped in water occasionally during boiling, to prevent crystals forming. Remove from heat and dip pan immediately into cold water to stop the cooking.

Tilt the pan slightly and dip the apples one at a time into the mixture. Lift out and twirl over the pan once or twice until evenly coated with toffee. Place on an oiled baking sheet until the toffee has hardened.
Makes 14

POPCORNETS

8 tablespoons corn oil
125 g (4 oz) popcorn kernels
4 tablespoons clear honey

Heat 2 tablespoons oil in a large heavy-based pan over high heat. Add a quarter of the corn, cover and cook, shaking the pan constantly, until the kernels have popped. Remove from the heat, pour over 1 tablespoon of the honey and stir thoroughly until coated. Transfer to a bowl and repeat with remaining popcorn. Spoon into paper cornets to serve.
Makes 14
To make paper cornets: Cut 30 cm (12 inch) squares of paper. Fold in half diagonally and crease firmly. Turn the two creased points in to meet the third point and secure along the join with sticky tape.

MAYPOLE

*4-egg Victoria
    sandwich cake
    mixture (see
    page 150)
175 g (6 oz) yellow
    butter icing (see
    page 150)
50 g (2 oz) apricot
    glaze (see page
    150)
500 g (1 lb) yellow
    moulding icing
    (see page 151)
125 g (4 oz) deep,
    yellow glacé icing
    (see page 150)
1 stick barley sugar
sugar flowers*

Line and grease a 25 cm (10 inch) round cake tin. Turn the mixture into the tin and bake in a preheated moderate oven, 180°C (350°F), Gas Mark 4, for 35 to 40 minutes. Turn onto a wire rack to cool.

Split the cake in half and sandwich together with the butter icing. Brush the cake with the apricot glaze. Roll out the moulding icing thinly on a board dusted with cornflour to a 33 cm (13 inch) circle and use to cover the cake, see page 151.

Put the glacé icing into a greaseproof paper piping bag fitted with a No. 2 writing nozzle. Pipe 6 lines from the centre of the cake to the edge. Write a name in each triangle.

Attach ribbons to one end of the barley sugar. Press into the centre of the cake, allowing one ribbon to fall to each name. Decorate with sugar flowers.
Makes one maypole

MUSHROOM HOUSE

*4-egg Victoria
    sandwich cake
    mixture (see page
    150)
75 g (3 oz) chocolate
    butter icing (see
    page 150)
3 tablespoons apricot
    glaze (see page
    150)
250 g (8 oz) red
    moulding icing (see
    page 151)
liquorice allsorts
25 g (1 oz) green
    butter icing (see
    page 150)
1 marshmallow
hundreds and
    thousands
sugar flowers*

Cleanly remove one end from an empty 793 g (1 lb 12 oz) can and clean the can thoroughly. Grease and flour the can and a 1.2 litre (2 pint) ovenproof bowl. Turn the cake mixture into the containers, two-thirds filling the can. Level the surfaces.

Bake in a preheated moderate oven, 160°C (325°F), Gas Mark 3, for 50 minutes for the can and 55 to 60 minutes for the basin. Loosen round the edges with a long thin knife and turn out onto a wire rack to cool.

Cover the 'can' cake with chocolate butter icing, reserving 2 tablespoons, and place on a cake board. Brush the 'basin' cake with apricot glaze. Roll out the moulding icing thinly on a surface sprinkled with cornflour into a 28 cm (11 inch) circle. Lift onto a rolling pin and position over the basin cake. Mould to the cake, folding any excess underneath at the base. Carefully place this cake on top of the other one for the roof.

Cut liquorice allsorts into thin slices and stick onto the roof with a little glaze to make spots.

Make doors and windows from liquorice allsorts and a chimney from a black liquorice allsort and a marshmallow. Press into position. Use the reserved butter icing to pipe on window frames and door knobs.

Ice the board with green butter icing and rough up with a fork to represent grass. Make a path up to the door with small triangles of liquorice and hundreds and thousands. Decorate with sugar flowers.
Makes one mushroom house

Maypole Cake

POST BOX

2-egg Victoria
    sandwich cake
    mixture (see page
    150)
75 g (3 oz) apricot
    glaze (see page
    150)
250 g (8 oz) red
    moulding icing (see
    page 151)
1 large round biscuit
2-3 pieces of liquorice
    ribbon
25 g (1 oz) black or
    brown glacé icing
    (see page 150)
1 liquorice allsort
icing sugar, sifted
1 plastic robin
    (optional)

Cleanly remove one end from 2 empty 397 g (14 oz) cans. Clean the cans thoroughly, then grease and flour them. Two-thirds fill the cans with the cake mixture and bake in a preheated moderate oven, 160°C (325°F), Gas Mark 3, for 30 to 35 minutes. Loosen the cakes round the edge with a long thin knife, then turn out and cool on a wire rack.

Cut the rounded tops off the cakes and discard. Cut a 2.5 cm (1 inch) piece from one cake, shape into a dome and set aside. Sandwich the 2 cakes together with apricot glaze, then brush all over with glaze.

Roll out three quarters of the moulding icing thinly on a surface sprinkled with cornflour, to an oblong measuring 25 × 15 cm (10 × 6 inches) and trim the edges; reserve trimmings. Wrap icing round the cake and mould the join together with a palette knife.

Stick the shaped dome onto the biscuit with a little apricot glaze and brush with glaze. Roll out remaining icing into a 13 cm (5 inch) circle and use to cover the dome and biscuit. Place on top of the cake to form the post box top. Make ridges round the top, using the back of a knife.

Fix 2 pieces of liquorice ribbon around the base of the post box with glaze. Press a strip of liquorice ribbon in position near the top for the opening. Cut a lid for the opening from the moulding icing trimmings and press into position. Fix a liquorice allsort below the opening to represent the 'collection times' label. Pipe on a door and writing, using glacé icing.

Sprinkle with icing sugar to represent snow and position the robin on top, if using.
Makes one post box

Mushroom House Cake; Post Box Cake

BASIC RECIPES

For quantities different from those given here, simply increase or decrease the ingredients in proportion.

VICTORIA SANDWICH CAKE MIXTURE

250 g (8 oz) butter or
  margarine
250 g (8 oz) caster
  sugar
4 eggs
250 g (8 oz) self-
  raising flour, sifted
2 tablespoons hot
  water

Cream the fat and sugar together until light and fluffy. Beat in the eggs one at a time, adding a tablespoon of the flour with the second egg. Fold in the remaining flour with a metal spoon, then the hot water.

Turn the mixture into the prepared tin(s) and bake as directed, until the cakes spring back when lightly pressed.
Makes a 4-egg quantity
VARIATION
Chocolate: Blend 1 tablespoon cocoa powder with 2 tablespoons hot water. Cool slightly then beat in with the fat and sugar.

CHOCOLATE WHISKED SPONGE MIXTURE

3 large eggs
75 g (3 oz) caster
  sugar
50 g (2 oz) plain
  flour
1 tablespoon cocoa
  powder
1 tablespoon oil

Place the eggs and sugar in a bowl and whisk over a pan of simmering water until thick and mousse-like. Sift the flour with the cocoa and fold in, then fold in the oil.

Turn into a lined and greased 20 cm (8 inch) round cake tin. Bake in a preheated moderately hot oven, 190°C (375°F), Gas Mark 5, for 30 to 35 minutes. Cool on a wire rack.
Makes a 3-egg quantity

SHORTCRUST PASTRY

125 g (4 oz) plain
  flour
50 g (2 oz) butter or
  margarine
1 tablespoon iced
  water

Sift the flour into a bowl. Rub in the butter or margarine until the mixture resembles fine breadcrumbs. Add the water gradually and mix to a firm dough. Use as required.
Makes a 125 g (4 oz) quantity

APRICOT GLAZE

125 g (4 oz) apricot
  jam
2 tablespoons water
squeeze of lemon
  juice

Heat the jam and water in a small pan gently until dissolved. Add the lemon juice, then sieve and return to the pan. Simmer until syrupy. Use warm.
Makes 125 g (4 oz)

GLACÉ ICING

125 g (4 oz) icing
  sugar
1 tablespoon warm
  water (approx)
few drops of food
  colouring
  (optional)

Sift the icing sugar into a mixing bowl and gradually stir in the water. The icing should be thick enough to coat the back of the spoon thickly. Beat in any colouring; use immediately.
Makes a 125 g (4 oz) quantity

BUTTER ICING

125 g (4 oz) butter
250 g (8 oz) icing
  sugar, sifted
2 tablespoons milk
flavouring (see
  below) or few
  drops of food
  colouring
  (optional)

Beat the butter with half the icing sugar until smooth. Beat in the remaining icing sugar with the milk and flavouring or colouring if using.
Makes a 250 g (8 oz) quantity
FLAVOURINGS
Chocolate: Blend 2 tablespoons cocoa powder with 2 tablespoons boiling water. Cool, then add to the mixture with only 1 tablespoon milk.
Coffee: Replace 1 tablespoon milk with 1 tablespoon coffee essence.

MOULDING ICING

1 small egg white
1 rounded tablespoon
  liquid glucose
350 g (12 oz) icing
  sugar, sifted
  (approximately)
few drops of food
  colouring
  (optional)

Mix the egg white and glucose in a basin. Gradually add enough icing sugar to form a stiff paste. Turn onto a surface sprinkled with cornflour and knead until smooth. Wrap in cling film to prevent drying.

Before moulding icing is applied, the cake must be brushed with apricot glaze. Mould the icing to the cake by rubbing the surface with a circular movement, keeping the hands dusted with icing sugar. Work any surplus icing to the bottom of the cake and cut off; this can be used again.

Makes a 350 g (12 oz) quantity

TOMATO AND ORANGE SAUCE

1 bunch of spring
  onions
2 tablespoons oil
500 g (1 lb)
  tomatoes, skinned
  and chopped
  juice of 1 orange
1 tablespoon lemon
  juice
2 tablespoons tomato
  purée
salt and pepper

Chop the spring onions. Heat 1 tablespoon of the oil in a pan, add the spring onions and fry gently for 2 minutes. Drain well.

Put the tomatoes, onions, fruit juices, tomato purée and remaining oil in a food processor or an electric blender and work until combined.

Transfer to a serving bowl and season with salt and pepper to taste. Chill well. Serve with fried fish.

Makes about 450 ml (¾ pint)

FRENCH DRESSING

175 ml (6 fl oz) olive
  oil
4 tablespoons wine
  vinegar
1 teaspoon French
  mustard
1 clove garlic, crushed
1 teaspoon clear
  honey
salt and pepper

Put all the ingredients in a screw-topped jar, adding salt and pepper to taste. Shake well to blend before serving.

Makes 250 ml (8 fl oz)

VARIATIONS:
Mustard Dressing: Add 2 tablespoons Meaux mustard.
Garlic Dressing: Crush 4 cloves garlic and add to the ingredients.

French Dressing; Honey and Lemon Dressing

HONEY AND LEMON DRESSING

4 tablespoons lemon
  juice
2 tablespoons clear
  honey
3 tablespoons olive oil
salt and pepper

Put all the ingredients in a screw-topped jar, adding salt and pepper to taste. Shake well to blend before serving.

Makes 150 ml (¼ pint)

SALAD DRESSING

French dressing can be stored in a bottle for several weeks so it is worth making up a large quantity at a time. Yogurt, cream or egg-based dressings can be stored for several days in a sealed container in the refrigerator.

YOGURT DRESSING

150 g (5.2 oz)
  natural yogurt
1 clove garlic, crushed
1 tablespoon cider
  vinegar
1 teaspoon clear
  honey
salt and pepper

Place all the ingredients in a bowl, adding salt and pepper to taste, and mix thoroughly with a fork.
Makes about 150 ml (¼ pint)
VARIATION:
Herb Dressing: Place the above ingredients in an electric blender or food processor with 15 g (½ oz) parsley and 15 g (½ oz) mixed mint and chives. Blend on maximum speed for 1 to 2 minutes. Chill until required. Shake well before using.
Makes 250 ml (8 fl oz)

Avocado Dressing; Herb Dressing; Quick Mayonnaise

SOURED CREAM DRESSING

142 ml (5 fl oz)
  soured cream
1 tablespoon lemon
  juice
1 clove garlic, crushed
1 teaspoon clear
  honey
salt and pepper
little milk (optional)

Place all the ingredients in a bowl, adding salt and pepper to taste, and mix thoroughly with a fork. Add milk to thin if necessary.
Makes 150 ml (¼ pint)
VARIATION:
Avocado Dressing: Place 1 peeled and chopped avocado pear, 5 tablespoons single cream and 1 teaspoon Worcestershire sauce in an electric blender or food processor. Blend until smooth, then mix with the soured cream dressing.
Makes 350 ml (12 fl oz)

QUICK MAYONNAISE

1 egg
½ teaspoon salt
½ teaspoon pepper
½ teaspoon mustard
  powder
2 teaspoons wine
  vinegar
150 ml (¼ pint)
  olive oil
150 ml (¼ pint)
  sunflower oil

Place the egg, seasonings and vinegar in an electric blender or food processor and blend on medium speed for a few seconds. Still on medium speed, add the oils drop by drop to begin with, through the lid, then in a thin stream as the mixture thickens.
   Store in an airtight container in the refrigerator for up to 10 days.
Makes about 300 ml (½ pint)
VARIATIONS:
Tomato Mayonnaise: Skin, seed and chop 2 tomatoes and place in the blender with 1 crushed clove garlic, ½ teaspoon brown sugar and 2 teaspoons tomato purée. Blend on maximum speed for 30 seconds, then stir into half the mayonnaise.
Makes about 250 ml (8 fl oz)

Traditional Method Mayonnaise:
Replace the 1 egg with 2 egg yolks. Beat the egg yolks and seasonings together in a bowl. Add the oils drop by drop, beating constantly. As the mixture thickens, add the oils in a steady stream. Add the vinegar and mix thoroughly.

VINAIGRETTE DRESSING

175 ml (6 fl oz)
  olive oil
4 tablespoons cider
  vinegar
1 teaspoon clear
  honey
1 clove garlic, crushed
2 tablespoons
  chopped mixed
  herbs (mint,
  parsley, chives,
  thyme)
salt and pepper

Put all the ingredients in a screw-topped jar, adding salt and pepper to taste. Shake well to blend before using.

Makes 250 ml (8 fl oz)

VARIATION:

Lemon or Lime Vinaigrette: Use 4 tablespoons fresh lemon or lime juice in place of the cider vinegar.

MINT AND HONEY DRESSING

2 tablespoons clear
  honey
4 tablespoons cider
  vinegar
3 tablespoons olive oil
1 tablespoon chopped
  mint
salt and pepper

Put all the ingredients in a screw-topped jar, adding salt and pepper to taste. Shake well to blend before serving.

Makes 150 ml (¼ pint)

SOY SAUCE DRESSING

175 ml (6 fl oz)
  sunflower oil
4 tablespoons soy
  sauce
2 tablespoons lemon
  juice
1 clove garlic, crushed
salt and pepper

Put all the ingredients in a screw-topped jar, adding salt and pepper to taste. Shake well to blend.

Makes 300 ml (½ pint)

VARIATIONS:

Ginger Dressing: Add a 2.5 cm (1 inch) piece peeled and finely chopped root ginger to the ingredients.

Chilli Dressing: Add 1 seeded and finely chopped green chilli.

Vinaigrette Dressing; Mint and Honey Dressing; Ginger Dressing

ENTERTAINING RECORD

If you wish to serve imaginative, never repetitive menus then you may wish to consider keeping a record of your parties for future reference. Record the party given, the date, who came and what was served. It is also handy to keep a note of which dishes were particularly successful and to have a reminder of any individual's likes or dislikes. These notes should prove very useful when choosing a menu for a forthcoming event.

INDEX

ACKNOWLEDGMENTS

The publishers would like to thank the following individuals who were involved in the preparation of material for this book:

All photography by Paul Williams, except pages 30, 31, 40, 42-3, 72-5, 100-2, and 104 by Bryce Attwell; 41 and 45 by Charlie Stebbings; and page 44 by Roger Phillips

Photographic stylists: Penny Markham, Roisin Nield, Liz Hippisley

Food for photography prepared by Carole Handslip, Caroline Ellwood, Clare Ferguson, Heather Lambert and Liz and Pete

Designed by Sue Storey